Thriving in the Spirit

Burton J. Campbell

OPEN BIBLE
CHURCHES

Thriving in the Spirit

Rev. Burton J. Campbell, Author
Rev. Randall A. Bach, General Editor
Dr. David L. Cole, Theological Editor
Rev. Andrea P. Johnson, Copy Editor

Copyright © 2023 by OBC Publishing
Published in Des Moines, Iowa, by OBC Publishing

ISBN: 9798392814435

All rights reserved. No portions of this book may be reproduced, stored in a retrieval system, or transmitted in any form by any means – electronic, mechanical, recording, or any other – except for brief quotations in reviews or articles, without the prior permission of the publisher.

Scripture quotations are from the Holy Bible, New International Version, unless otherwise indicated. Copyright 1973, 1978, 1984 by International Bible Society.

Cover design by Chris Cavan
Book design and layout by Greg Roberts

Printed in the United States of America
First Edition 2023

Contents

	Preface	V
	Acknowledgments	VII
	Introduction: Welcome to Thriving in the Spirit	IX
Part 1	The Ministry of the Spirit in the Believer	1
Chapter 1	Jesus and the Spirit	5
Chapter 2	The Baptism in the Holy Spirit	13
Chapter 3	The Spirit Working in Us	27
Chapter 4	Speaking in Tongues	39
Part 2	The Ministry of the Spirit in the Local Church	53
Chapter 5	Embracing the Move of the Spirit: Lessons from the Church in Jerusalem	57
Chapter 6	Following the Move of the Spirit: From Jerusalem to Antioch	65
Chapter 7	Growing in our Experience of the Spirit: The Church in Ephesus	75
Chapter 8	Guidelines for Spirit-Empowered Ministry: The Church in Corinth	85
Chapter 9	The Ministry of the Spirit and Extra-Biblical Phenomena	99
Epilogue	Further Up and Further In	115

IV

Preface

The Holy Spirit has never allowed Himself to be placed inside a box. From the Reformation through the Great Awakening, from Azusa Street to the Charismatic Renewal, and throughout every historical era and event, the Spirit of God has operated consistently with God the Father's directives and His Word.

From the time the Holy Spirit descended upon humankind in a new dimension as recorded in Acts 2, as a violent rushing wind that filled the house with tongues of fire and with the disciples speaking in other tongues, people have attempted to both understand and sometimes manage or direct the work of the Spirit. At other times, people have attempted to stop or build walls around the Spirit. But John 3:8 makes clear that the Holy Spirit, symbolized by wind, *"blows wherever it pleases. You hear its sound, but you cannot tell where it comes from or where it is going."*

The Holy Spirit does not need to be and will not be managed. Rather, we must manage ourselves and our response to the Spirit. Incorrect instruction, self-asserting mannerisms, and faulty leadership can act as barriers, sow confusion, and hinder people from receiving the fullness of the Holy Spirit and flowing with Him. Open Bible Churches was founded on a passionate love for and hunger to receive every facet of the Holy Spirit's power. That remains our commitment. The purpose of *Thriving in the Spirit* is simply to return to what the Word of

God instructs us about this dynamic component of the Trinity's activity. Burt Campbell is the gifted writer who leads our exploration of the Spirit in this book. We owe a debt of gratitude to Burt for devoting himself to this project. Times change. People change. Cultures change. Churches change. However, the Holy Spirit stays faithfully true to His Sovereign purpose throughout these epic changes while at the same time remaining fresh with each new season. Indeed, the wind of the Spirit blows. His Spirit is never stale, and He defies our ability to predict His direction.

Acts 2:17 declares, *"'In the last days,' God says, 'I will pour out my Spirit upon all people.'"* Are you ready? Do you long to thrive in the Holy Spirit? If so, join us in this biblical, practical tour of promises and instruction about the Spirit and how we should respond to Him. Remember this: whatever portion of the Holy Spirit that now is resident in you, there is more available!

Randall A. Bach, President
Open Bible Churches

Acknowledgments

Thriving in the Spirit is a resource that has been a long time in the making, and it is the product of numerous people who have worked diligently to help make this book a reality. Though it bears my name as author, there are many others whose thoughts, questions, and interactions have served to help me write with greater clarity and focus. I am deeply indebted to the following people who provided reviews and feedback: Rev. Josh Bingaman, Dr. David L. Cole, Rev. Michael W. Juntunen, Rev. Deodath Mathai, Rev. Jorge L. Morelles, Rev. Joshua P. Stelly, and Rev. Sarah E. Williams. Their comments have been of enormous value in refining this material. In addition, I must also note that Dr. Cole first started grading my papers in the late 1980s while I was one of his Systematic Theology students at Oral Roberts University. He wouldn't let me get away with substandard work as I was learning to become a more disciplined student back then, and I am grateful for his encouraging words and thoughtful critique today.

Andrea Johnson has painstakingly poured over this material, not only fixing typographical errors and adjusting grammar, but also coordinating reviews and revisions and then reformatting my final submissions for publication. Her expertise has certainly enhanced the flow and readability of what I have tried to present. Thank you so much, Andrea! Trudy Kutz also kindly and thoroughly proofread this material. I appreciate her "catches," which have enhanced the clarity of this material.

The support of my darling wife, Linda, has been invaluable, not only as I have spent long hours fixed on this task, but in every aspect of life and ministry. Her ongoing love and commitment mean the world to me, and I am ever grateful to journey alongside her.

I am deeply humbled to have been asked by Open Bible President Randall Bach to take on this project. I so appreciate his heart for Open Bible Churches and his desire to champion the work of the Holy Spirit within our ministry family. I am truly appreciative of his tireless efforts to provide encouragement, secure feedback, and offer support. His patience and gentle prodding during long stretches when I was inundated with pressures from both work and graduate studies helped to keep me on track until this book was completed.

I love Open Bible Churches. I am thankful for the history of our movement and remain hopeful and eager as our future unfolds. We were forged and established in the fires of Spirit-filled ministry. Over the decades that have since transpired, there have been countless stories of how the Holy Spirit has continued to advance the kingdom of God and brought transformation to people all around the world. May that joyous work have been just the beginning of all He will yet do through Open Bible, and may this book help inspire a yearning for more.

To the Father, Son, and Spirit, to You be all praise and glory. May this text serve Your Church and bring encouragement and strength to many. I remain grateful to serve.

Burton J. Campbell
June 2023

Introduction

Welcome to a new life in Christ, a thriving participation with the Spirit of God! The Bible says, *"Anyone who belongs to Christ has become a new person. The old life is gone; a new life has begun!"* (2 Corinthians 5:17, NLT). For some people that change is experienced immediately and dramatically. For others, the change is noticed more slowly over time as inner peace and new thought processes are developed. For everyone, however, that change is accomplished by the power of the Holy Spirit working in us. He is constantly in motion, leading us into all truth and bringing us into deeper relationship with Himself. Living in relationship with Him is the greatest adventure of any lifetime.

Here is a truth: there is a world more real than the one we see with our physical eyes. We are each part of it whether we realize it or not. The spiritual plane exists, not merely as a concept of heaven, "up there, somewhere," but rather it is all around us, all at once. Jesus called it the "kingdom of God." Throughout time, people have been touched by it, and the Bible records many of these encounters. Part of living out a new life in Christ includes becoming aware of and interacting in this spiritual realm by embracing a relationship with the Holy Spirit.

In Genesis 28, Jacob traveled back to his mother's home country to find a wife. On the first night of his journey, as he fell asleep, he had a dream from God.

The dream involved a large staircase between heaven and earth (some biblical translations call it a "ladder"). On the stairway were angels moving up and down, traveling back and forth. In that moment, Jacob experienced a blessing from God and a promise that the Lord would be with him until all His purposes were accomplished. Jacob was destined for a life bigger than he could fathom, and Father God invited him to embrace the possibilities found in pursuing that destiny.

What Jacob encountered in his dream was the intersection of the spiritual realm and the physical world, and we also are meant to live in the experience of this same junction. It is the place where the presence and power of the kingdom of God at work in the midst of the everyday life brings impact in a tangible way. As in Jacob's dream, we can become aware of and interact with this unseen reality. The Bible, which contains not just the history of God's dealing with humankind but God's very Word to us, serves as our source for understanding and experiencing the workings of the Spirit as the Lord continues to uphold and fulfill His promises. It verifies that as believers in Jesus we are meant for a life of far greater reach than we may otherwise envision because of the reality of the Spirit of God living within us.

This new life is not necessarily one of fame or fortune. It is not measured by outward symbols of status or success. Vocations, wealth, material possessions, and fame all are incidental to the ultimate purposes of God. His intentions for us are certainly much more. Choosing to surrender to Christ as Lord means we are willing to give up our old way of living with its earthly goals and ambitions and embrace a new life empowered by the Spirit of God. He cares about our needs, He cares about our desires, and He can be trusted. His thoughts are higher than ours, His ways are higher than our ways, and He is always good.

The prophet Jeremiah makes known the heart of God for His people as he writes, *"'For I know the plans I have for you,' says the Lord. 'They are plans for good and not for disaster, to give you a future and a hope'"* (Jeremiah 29:11, NLT). What God does is right. Everything He does is ultimately for the good of humankind, and He calls each of us to be part of His work. If we are willing, our lives can resound with incredible influence and impact regardless of our station or occupation. God gave the Israelites, whom Jeremiah prophesied would become captives of Babylon, a future and a hope by sustaining them in the midst of their captivity for seventy years.

God is looking to sustain us in this life as well through a vibrant relationship with the Holy Spirit. A life lived in loving cooperation and relationship with the Spirit of God is one full of the satisfaction found by finally being made complete in Him. It is not about outward accomplishment or worldly success; it is about being found in Christ and discovering His way of living day in and day out. That kind of life changes the world, one relationship at a time.

God is not distant. He is not merely watching from afar, aloof and uninvolved. He is present amid everyday circumstances, ministering His love, compassion, comfort, healing, correction, mercy, and more. Although He is omnipresent (everywhere at once), omniscient (all-knowing), and omnipotent (all-powerful), He is also omnisapient (all-wise)! In His wisdom, He chooses to work first and foremost in the hearts and lives of people. The Apostle Paul writes to the followers of Christ in Romans 8:11 (NLT), *"The Spirit of God, who raised Jesus from the dead, lives in you."* As carriers of His presence, believers in Jesus are meant to touch all those around them with the Lord's love and power. This happens through prayer, kindness, service, sacrifice, compassion, forgiveness, and genuine love. Along the way, God works supernaturally and miraculously through the outpouring of spiritual gifts and encounters. What an exciting and meaningful way to live!

The Lord has a destiny for each of us. Though it may involve certain goals and objectives, it goes well beyond the outward things we do. He is making us into new people. Romans 8:29 (NLT) declares, *"For God knew his people in advance, and he chose them to become like his Son."* God has intentions for our lives. He wants to make us look just like Jesus. Can you imagine your life impacting others the same way Jesus did? As you look in the mirror now, you might see only your weaknesses, limitations, and shortcomings. God is not daunted by any of that. He sees the reality of His Kingdom taking shape inside of us, transforming us from the inside out as Christ is formed in us and the Spirit of God saturates us from the inside out. We are meant to live this life under His guidance and minister to others supernaturally by His power.

This book is intended to serve as an introduction to this kind of Spirit-filled life. It is by no means exhaustive or to be understood as any kind of "final say" on the subject. It is a primer, a way to begin; it is a way to learn to thrive in this new life in the Spirit. Hopefully it will help answer common questions about who the Spirit is and how He works in our lives. Sometimes people carry misconceptions about the ministry of the Holy Spirit that stem from past experiences or misunderstood teaching. In the pages that follow, you will find some helpful explorations through the Scripture that work to lovingly address those misunderstandings.

This resource is also meant to help leaders, churches, and other ministries think through guidelines and healthy practices that foster and encourage the work of the Holy Spirit in their midst. The hope is to empower churches to embrace a framework that actively promotes the development of spiritual fruit and the deployment of spiritual gifts across their congregations. In some churches the Holy Spirit can seem like an almost forgotten member of the Trinity. As for us, let's consider how we might celebrate His presence and become intentional about letting Him have His way. As we encourage believers to embrace new life in the Spirit, may our churches strive to offer loving, balanced, dynamic instruction that helps people to experience the richness of vibrant Spirit-filled living.

As you make your way through this book, ask the Lord to help you to do more than just read the words in print. Instead, interact with the material, discuss its concepts among your family and friends, and incorporate its application into your daily life. Consider how these teachings and discussions can contribute to better and best practices as your church conducts ministry. Wrestle through what is presented until it is your own. Here's how:

As you read each chapter, ask the Holy Spirit to reveal Himself to you. Highlight or underline portions that He seems to emphasize as you read. Add notes in the margins to include your reflections and inspirations.

Look up the many scripture references in your Bible. Consider both the preceding and following scriptural passages. What is the context for these verses? What is the life situation being described? How would the original readers have understood the writing? What key words, phrases, and characters stand out to you? What timeless message does the passage have for today?

Note that each chapter includes opportunities to deliberately pause and reflect on what has been presented and then to work through some important questions. Consider working through these in a separate journal or in discussion with a close friend and follower of Jesus. Though this book certainly is informational, let it become something transformational by your engaging and wrestling through the challenges and opportunities it presents.

Look for ways to live what you read every day. As you become increasingly aware of the presence and power of the Holy Spirit around you, choose to become an active participant with Him in ministering the goodness of God to others.

In his book *The Great Divorce* (a spiritual allegory about the nature and reality of heaven and hell), C.S. Lewis writes, *"Heaven is not a state of mind. Heaven is reality itself. All that is fully real is heavenly. For all that can be shaken will be shaken and only the unshakeable remains."* It is time to awaken to the reality of a supernatural life in the Spirit. Ask the Lord to shake you right now from all that is false and limited and to open your eyes to see, experience, and embrace the fullness of His blessing and promises for your life.

God's Kingdom is real. It is more real than anything else we know, and it is all around us. Come join in the adventure. Welcome to *Thriving in the Spirit.*

Burton J. Campbell

Part 1
The Ministry of the Spirit in the Believer

God has always desired that we would know Him personally. He is not merely watching us from a distance; He is intricately involved in the day-to-day aspects of our lives. He cares about our pain. He works to heal our hurts. Through the power of forgiveness, He offers cleansing from all that separates us from Him and from one another. He nudges us and orchestrates our steps so that we might fulfill His plans and purposes for us. He fills our hearts with His goodness and with character traits that come directly from Him that help us to better demonstrate His love to the world. He shows us what is true and right and helps us to grow, deepen, and develop our faith more and more as we trust in Him. He does all of this by the power and presence of the Holy Spirit in our lives.

Jesus called twelve disciples to come and follow Him. That didn't mean they just showed up for meetings on the Sabbath or for midweek prayer sessions on Wednesday nights. Rather, they lived in continual, ongoing relationship together. The disciples didn't learn from Jesus only by listening to His teachings, but also by observing His life and actions up close and personal, day after day. They engaged in ministry and life . . . together.

During His last night with them before going to the cross, Jesus made them a promise:

> **And I will ask the Father, and he will give you another Counselor to be with you forever – the Spirit of truth. The world cannot accept him, because it neither sees him nor knows him. But you know him, for he lives with you and will be in you (John 14:16-17).**

Jesus let them know that even though He was about to leave them, He was not abandoning them. They would not be alone. Just as they had been intimately involved with one another in a personal way, they would have a similar relationship with the Holy Spirit. The Spirit would be with them and in them!

A personal relationship with the Holy Spirit is meant to be an essential aspect of the Christian life. The Spirit guides us into all truth. He shows us things to come. He takes the words of Jesus and makes them plain for us. He reproduces the character of Christ in us. He empowers us in supernatural ways that both strengthen us internally and enable us to effectively reach others with the love of God. We are meant to live out this earthly life centered in a continual and personal relationship with Him.

This is the focus of Part One of this book. It comprises the first four chapters of this book and is intended to help us discover and explore various aspects of a personal relationship with the Holy Spirit. As we read, pray, and reflect, may we discover the wonders of His presence anew.

4 THE MINISTRY OF THE SPIRIT IN THE BELIEVER

Chapter 1
Jesus and the Spirit

Our experience of life in the Spirit begins with Jesus. The Bible is very clear that without knowing Christ as Lord, we are all "dead" in our sins (Ephesians 2:1, Colossians 2:13). When we trust in Jesus as Lord, believing that God raised Him from the dead, a miracle takes place, and we are made alive! (Ephesians 2:4-10). The Bible says it's like being born again. This is all made possible by the death and resurrection of Jesus, and it happens in the moment by the presence and power of the Holy Spirit. Romans 8:11 (NLT) says, *"The Spirit of God, who raised Jesus from the dead, lives in you. And just as God raised Christ Jesus from the dead, he will give life to your mortal bodies by this same Spirit living within you."* What a powerful picture that is! We pass from death into life by the work of the Holy Spirit on the inside of us!

THE BREATH OF GOD

It is the Holy Spirit who gave humankind life in the very beginning in a cooperative work with the Father and the Son. In Genesis 1:2 we are told that as God was creating the heavens and the earth, the Spirit of God hovered over the waters. The Hebrew word for "spirit" also includes the idea of "breath" or "wind." It is fascinating, then, to realize that when God formed humanity from the dust of the earth that God breathed into that first man the *breath of life* (Genesis 2:7). It was only then that Adam came alive. More than just physical properties and biological components, Adam needed the breath of God, His Spirit, to be empowered with life.

This idea of the Spirit giving new life is also seen in the New Testament. After Jesus was raised from the dead, He suddenly appeared to His disciples that same evening as they were gathered together. What a night of utter joy and amazement that had to be for all His disciples! John's gospel records that the Lord then commissioned His followers for ministry by saying, *"As the Father has sent me, I am sending you"* (John 20:21). For what purpose had the Father sent Jesus? According to what Jesus Himself declared in Luke 4:18-19, His mission was to preach good news to the poor. He was sent to proclaim freedom for prisoners and recovery of sight for the blind. He came to set the oppressed free and to proclaim the year of the Lord's favor. The desire of the Father included the hope that all who believed in Jesus would not perish but instead have eternal life (John 3:16). It is with this same mindset and hope that Jesus sends His disciples, including each of us, into the world. Jesus did not merely commission His followers with words, He also chose to empower them by pouring out the Holy Spirit to each one.

As Jesus was speaking, John records that He *"breathed on them and said, 'Receive the Holy Spirit'"* (John 20:22). Isn't that wild? It follows a pattern that is reminiscent of the original creation of humankind. In fact, the Apostle Paul declared in his letter to the Colossians, that it is by the Lord Jesus that all things were created (Colossians 1:16). In much the same way that the Lord breathed into the dust of the earth and brought forth life, Jesus breathed on the disciples so that they would receive the Holy Spirit and be empowered for this new life of ministry. If disciples are going to be sent into the world just as Jesus was, then they need to be empowered in the same way Jesus was. That raises a couple of questions for us to consider: How is it that Jesus was empowered to accomplish the things He did? Are we really empowered to minister in the same way He did? To get our heads around all that, let's reflect for a moment on the nature of Jesus.

HOW JESUS LIVED AND MINISTERED

The Bible is quite clear that Jesus is God, who took on flesh and lived among us (John 1:14). Part of the wonder of God is that He exists in the divine relationship of a three-part unity: God the Father, God the Son, and God the Holy Spirit. They are ever connected and part of one another and each fully complete with one another. Theologians call this the "Trinity." Being one with the Father in every way, Jesus, the Son of God, therefore possesses all the divine attributes of God, and the Scripture is full of many examples of this.

During His last supper in the upper room with His disciples, Jesus told them that if anyone has seen Him, they have also seen the Father (John 14:9). The Apostle Paul later wrote that the fullness of all Deity lives in bodily form in the person of Jesus (Colossians 1:19, 2:9). We've already also mentioned above that Paul presents the truth that Jesus is the Creator of all things (Colossians 1:16). In other words, all of the acts of creation performed by God and mentioned in Genesis include the active participation of the preincarnate Son as well. Moreover, the book of Revelation makes it clear that Jesus is the Almighty, the one *"who is, and who was, and who is to come"* (Revelation 1:8). Scripturally, there is no question that Jesus is God.

Yet when Jesus walked the earth He also truly lived as a man. Yes, He was certainly and fully God, but during His earthly ministry He opted to live under the limitations of humanity. Without question, He was completely human in every way. Paul elaborates on this when he writes that Jesus *"being in very nature God, did not consider equality with God something to be grasped, but made himself nothing, taking the very nature of a servant, being made in human likeness. And being found in appearance as a man, he humbled himself and became obedient to death – even death on a cross!"* (Philippians 2:6-8). In other words, Jesus didn't live and minister among us by the power of His divine attributes, but rather subjected Himself to living with the same limitations as the rest of us. This doesn't mean that He somehow stopped being divine or that He no longer had access to His godly attributes, but rather that He chose not to make use of them while living here on earth. He voluntarily took on the role of a lowly servant as a human being. How is it then that He demonstrated such great obedience, compassion, wisdom, healings, miracles, and more? He relied on the Holy Spirit.

Before Jesus ever launched into ministry, the Gospel writers tell us that He came before his cousin, John the Baptist, to be baptized in the Jordan River. John preached a baptism of repentance for the forgiveness of sins. Jesus, however, did not have any need for repentance or forgiveness. His baptism served a different purpose. The Bible declares that as Jesus was praying and being baptized, heaven was opened, and the Holy Spirit descended on Him in the form of a dove. It was after being baptized in the Spirit in this way that Jesus' ministry began (Luke 3:23). The immediate impact of all this on the life and ministry of Jesus was soon apparent. The Scripture records that Jesus was now *"led by the Spirit"* into the wilderness (Luke 4:1) and that He returned *"in the power of the Spirit"* (Luke 4:14).

So, all that Jesus said and did throughout His earthly ministry was accomplished through His relationship with the Holy Spirit. Everything was done by the power of the Spirit. By the Spirit's power He proclaimed the kingdom of God, healed the sick, ministered in compassion, performed miracles, confounded His critics, and endured and overcame the hardships of this life. In this way, Christ serves as the model for all who follow Him, and that includes us!

Part of the Gospel message is the truth that Jesus is God who came in the flesh. As we look at Him, we are meant to see what the Father is like (Colossians 1:15). However, another part of the Gospel message is the truth that Jesus is fully human and the ideal person. As we look at Him, we also must learn to see our potential, our design, and our hope. Just as Adam in the beginning was given life by the breath of God and was created to be in divine relationship with the Father, we too bear this same imprint of God over us. We are meant to be filled with the Spirit of God and to live out our relationship with Him in a way that is intimate, personal, and overwhelmingly infectious to the world. Along the way, we are thereby empowered to lovingly minister to others in supernatural ways.

THE PERSON OF THE SPIRIT

Sometimes, if we are not careful, images in our culture rather than the Word of God can unduly influence our understanding of the Holy Spirit. For example, in 1977 George Lucas released *Star Wars* and suddenly launched a cultural phenomenon. Today, that franchise has resulted in a myriad of ever-expanding films, multiple animated and live-action television series, and countless books, comics, and related merchandise. Societal fascination has only increased with the creation of Disney theme parks devoted to the *Star Wars* legend and the promise of many films yet to come. Looming in the background of every *Star Wars* story is a concept that Lucas called "the Force." This science fiction idea holds that the Force is an energy field that surrounds all of creation and indwells every living being to various degrees. It provides moments of special direction and supernatural-like power that enables the user to accomplish amazing feats. I was only nine years old when that first film was released, but I remember church members having multiple conversations about how "the Force" was much like the Holy Spirit. Their intentions were good. They were trying to find contemporary ways for expressing truths about the Holy Spirit, but their depictions were being shaped by the culture instead of the Scripture. Unfortunately, many people today, even in the church, persist in this view of the Spirit, as if He were some kind of mystical, cosmic energy that we can somehow tap into for our personal use. The Holy Spirit, however, is not an impersonal power source that somehow enables believers in Christ to develop miraculous abilities. He is not a "Force."

The Holy Spirit is a person. He's one of the three divine Persons, along with the Father and the Son, who comprise the fullness of God. The Spirit has force and is absolutely powerful, but He cannot be relegated to simply being a force or a power. *He* is not an *"it."* Again, He is a person. He acts as He sees fit and in perfect accordance with the will of God. Throughout the Scripture He is predominately referred to as "the Spirit" or "the Holy Spirit," but He also bears many other titles that all reveal something about His character and His attributes.

The Bible calls Him "the Spirit of God," "the Spirit of the Lord," and "the Spirit of the Sovereign Lord." In a prophecy regarding how the Spirit will rest upon the Messiah, Isaiah uses multiple titles including "the Spirit of wisdom and understanding," "the Spirit of counsel and might," and "the Spirit of the knowledge of the fear of the Lord" (Isaiah 11:2). Jesus also calls Him "the Spirit

> **PAUSE AND REFLECT:**
>
> As you read through the various titles given to the Holy Spirit, what do they suggest to you about Him?
>
> What does it mean that He is "holy"?
>
> Why do you think Isaiah uses words like "wisdom," "understanding," "counsel," "knowledge," and "fear of the Lord" all in connection to the Spirit of God?
>
> As Jesus uses the term "Advocate" to describe the Holy Spirit, He uses a legal term. The idea of an advocate is a person close to the situation who can plead someone's case before a judge. How does this impact your understanding of the work of the Spirit in your life?

of the Father," "the Spirit of truth," and "the Advocate" (some translations say "Comforter"). The Apostle Paul additionally refers to Him as "the Spirit of Christ," "the Spirit of Him who raised Jesus from the dead," and "the Spirit of His Son." Other passages call Him "the eternal Spirit," "the Spirit of grace," and "the Spirit of glory."

Notice how many of these various references connect Him with both the Father and with Jesus in clear demonstration of the Trinity. The variety of names also reveals much to us about His character and His attributes. The Bible tells us that the Spirit took an active role in creation, endues people with power, leads and guides us into all truth, convicts us of sin, reminds us of all that Jesus has said, demonstrates fruit (godly characteristics) through us, enables many kinds of spiritual gifts, and more. He indwells the life of every believer, and He can be grieved when we choose to hold on to our sinful ways and mindsets.

LIVING AS JESUS LIVED

Just as Jesus lived by the guidance and the power of the Holy Spirit as found in a relationship with Him, we are meant to do the same. Paul told the Galatian believers that they were to *"walk by the Spirit"* (Galatians 5:16, ESV). He goes on to say, *"Since we live in the Spirit, let us keep in step with the Spirit"* (Galatians 5:25). Every person who has given themselves over to the lordship of Jesus is meant to awaken to an ongoing relationship with the Holy Spirit who fills our lives with His presence and then works mightily through us to impact the world around us. Some Christians believe that this outpouring of the Spirit is just for some Christians. They mistakenly believe that His presence is supposed to manifest in powerful ways only through those who are somehow especially called to vocational ministry. They haven't realized that He wants to work deeply in and through all of us. On the day of Pentecost, Peter declared to the crowd that in these last days God is pouring out His Spirit on all people, both men and women, both young and old. No one is left out.

God, who dwells in the continual relationship of the divine union of the Father, Son, and Spirit, has invited us to participate in that relationship as well. He calls us to know Him by the Spirit, to be filled with His presence, and to live out of the overflow of our relationship with Him, touching others with His goodness and love. Like a sponge filled with water, He wants to saturate us with His

Spirit so that we might spill out and impact all with whom we come in contact. Just as Jesus lived empowered by the Spirit and showcased the kingdom of God to others, we are enabled to do the same. To experience the full potential of that kind of life, we need the baptism in the Holy Spirit – a topic we will explore in the next chapter.

> **PAUSE AND REFLECT:**
>
> What do you think of the idea that Jesus ministered out of His relationship with the Holy Spirit while He was on earth? What do you think of the idea that as we look at Him, we are meant to see both what God is like and also what humanity is meant to be like?
>
> Why does it matter that we understand that the Spirit is a person and not just some divine energy force?
>
> Do you believe that Jesus is sending you out to live just as He did in order that the world might experience the Gospel message for themselves? What feelings and hopes are stirred in you by that thought?

12 JESUS AND THE SPIRIT

Chapter 2
The Baptism in the Holy Spirit

People often have lots of questions regarding what the Bible calls the "baptism in the Holy Spirit." Acts 1:5 records Jesus' words to His disciples that *"John baptized with water, but in a few days you will be baptized with the Holy Spirit."* There is much to consider about this incredible and powerful statement.

The word "baptized" that is used in this verse is translated from the Greek word *"baptizo."* It means to be "immersed" or "saturated." In the Gospels, John the Baptist was so named because he called people to repent of their sins and then fully baptized them in the Jordan River as an outward sign of their repentance. Jesus uses this same word to describe being saturated/immersed with the person of the Holy Spirit.

The reference to water baptism is used by Jesus in the above Acts passage as an illustration of what He desires to do in us by His Spirit. It has been said that in those days when people were baptized in water, they would go under completely with their mouths open. The intention was that they were being completely purified and filled, inside and out. That kind of baptism was meant to symbolize repentance and cleansing from sin. In similar fashion, we still baptize Christ-followers in water to publicly recognize their confession of Christ. Christian baptism provides us with a picture of being crucified and buried with Christ, and then resurrected into new life. Believers in Jesus are made new from the inside out, cleansed and transformed, and brought into right standing with God. The Bible uses this picture of immersion in water to help us understand the baptism in the Holy Spirit. Through Spirit baptism, the Lord wants to cause us to be saturated thoroughly with the Spirit of God.

People utilize many different terms to describe this act of God, using phrases like "the infilling of the Spirit," "the baptism in the Spirit," or "receiving the Spirit." Generally, when we talk about receiving the "baptism in the Holy Spirit," we are referring to one's initial experience of being saturated by the Spirit of God. When we first confess Jesus as the Lord of our lives (when we believe that Jesus is the Son of God, place our faith in His death on the cross to cleanse us from our sins, and surrender ourselves completely over to Him), the Bible says that Christ will come and live in us by His Spirit (Romans 8:10-11). The Spirit of God comes into our lives in a transformational way at that very moment and rescues us from the effects of sin. We come alive! Yet that doesn't necessarily mean we've also been baptized in the Holy Spirit. Though these events can certainly happen simultaneously, they are often experienced separately. One can drink a glass of water and be nourished by it. In fact, a person could say that he or she has, in a real sense, "received it into their life," but that person is not saturated until he or she is completely plunged beneath the surface of the water. Additionally, Scripture is filled with several examples of believers in Christ who experienced the baptism in the Spirit as an event separate from when they first believed in Christ.

"YOU WILL RECEIVE POWER..."

Just before ascending to heaven, Jesus very clearly told His disciples to stay in Jerusalem until they experienced the baptism in the Spirit (see both Luke 24:49 and Acts 1:4). He described the baptism in the Spirit as a gift the Father had promised to give them. It is interesting to note in John 20:22 that the newly resurrected Jesus turned to His disciples when He first appeared to them, *breathed on them*, and then said, *"Receive the Holy Spirit."* Yet we also know that the first chapter in Acts indicates that these same disciples were also additionally instructed to stay and wait for the full unfolding of this promised baptism (saturation) in the Spirit.

In Acts 1:8, Jesus further explained to His disciples, *"You will receive power when the Holy Spirit comes on you, and you will be my witnesses in Jerusalem, and in all Judea and Samaria, and to the ends of the earth.*" The word "power" is translated from the Greek word "*dunamis*" and includes the idea of "might, strength, force, ability, capability, resources." Our English word "dynamite" comes from this Greek word. It conveys the ideas of mighty force, the power to make a difference. The Gospel writers use the same word to mean "miracle" or "miraculous power." This kind of power is given by the Spirit so that we can be an effective witness for Jesus. In the Greek translation of the Old Testament that was used during the time of Christ, the *LXX* (also known as the *Septuagint*), this Greek word is also used to describe both military force and the power of a ruler. In the Gospels, the word is used to describe the miracles of Jesus (Mark 6:2; Luke 19:37). It's a word used to indicate supernatural activity that makes a significant difference in the lives of people, powerfully advancing the kingdom of God!

We need the Spirit's power in order to demonstrate and maintain both a transformed life and a supernatural ministry that together serve to advance the Gospel message to the world. We need to be saturated with the Holy Spirit so that His extraordinary character can come to the foreground of our lives and help us to live in such a way that God is continually glorified. The baptism in the Holy Spirit is also meant to have the effect of equipping us with supernatural power for the purpose of enabling us to be "witnesses" for Christ. Being a witness for Christ means being able to credibly testify to the reality of the risen Jesus through our words, actions, and lifestyle. We are meant to be a reflection of the ministry of Jesus, showcasing both His character (which Paul describes in Galatians 5:22-23 as the "fruit" of the Spirit), and His miraculous works, which are enabled by what Paul calls "gifts" of the Spirit and/or "gifts of grace" (see Romans 12:6-8; 1 Corinthians 12:4-11; and John 14:11-12).

The fruit of the Spirit is love, joy, peace, patience, kindness, goodness, faithfulness, gentleness, and self-control (Galatians 5:22-23). None of these characteristics originate in us. They come from the Spirit of God. In addition, the Holy Spirit operates supernatural gifts through our lives to effectively reach others and point them to the Father (1 Corinthians 12:4-12). The ability to bring healing, perform miracles, prophesy, and display other supernatural acts comes only from the presence of the Spirit as He saturates our lives.

> **PAUSE AND REFLECT:**
>
> - How have you been impacted by the fruit of the Spirit that was evident in the life of someone else?
>
> - In what ways did God work through others to help bring you to a place of faith in Him?
>
> - What has been your experience of seeing God supernaturally work through other believers? How was your life affected?
>
> - Why is it important that any emphasis on the baptism in the Holy Spirit include a focus on both the "fruit" of the Spirit and the "power" of the Spirit?

In Acts 2, we discover that the baptism in the Holy Spirit was first experienced quite dramatically and suddenly as the disciples were gathered in an upper room. The immediate effect of this outpouring of the Spirit was that the disciples began declaring the wonders of God in unknown tongues (Acts 2:11; for a larger discussion of speaking in tongues, see chapter 4). Additionally, Peter began to act with focused boldness, effectively preaching to thousands. The rest of the book of Acts then describes the ministry of the church through powerful witness, preaching, miracles, supernatural occurrences, and steadfast endurance.

SPIRIT BAPTISM IN THE SCRIPTURE

So how did people receive this baptism in the Holy Spirit? In Acts 1, the disciples were instructed to wait for it, but that doesn't mean they were just passively sitting and waiting. Rather, they met together and spent their time in unified prayer. In Acts 2:38, Peter told the crowd to whom he was preaching to *"repent and be baptized [in water], every one of you, in the name of Jesus Christ for the forgiveness of your sins. And you will receive the gift of the Holy Spirit."* By using the word "gift," it is apparent that Peter is referring to the same saturation of the Holy Spirit he himself had just experienced (the promised "gift" of the Father). Some Christians suggest that he is referring to a more generalized reception of the Spirit that comes with a surrender to the lordship of Christ, more akin to what the Apostle John described in his gospel (when Jesus said, *"Receive the Holy Spirit"* – John 20:22). We will look at additional scriptures for broader understanding as we consider them as a whole. It is notable, however, that the reception of the Spirit is repeatedly presented as a promise to all who repent and are baptized in the name of Jesus Christ, not just for the believers of that time but for all believers even today!

The next account of an outpouring of the Spirit in the book of Acts is found in chapter 4, verse 8: *"Then Peter, filled with the Holy Spirit, said to them . . . ."* Peter, having received the Holy Spirit and having been baptized in the Holy Spirit, is suddenly in the moment "filled up" with the Holy Spirit again and empowered to again give bold witness. **This statement implies that this initial baptism in the Spirit is meant to be combined with repeated "infillings."** Such thought would be in keeping with Paul's emphasis in Ephesians 5:18 for the church to literally "keep on being filled" with the Spirit and his instruction to Timothy to *"fan into flame the gift of God, which is in you"* (2 Timothy 1:6).

Another such filling was experienced by all the believers while they were gathered in prayer in Acts 4:31. The book of Acts also lists other accounts where believers who had already been baptized in the Spirit experience subsequent, sudden, additional infillings (see Acts 13:9 and 13:52). This tells us that the baptism in the Holy Spirit is not simply to be regarded as a one-time experience, but rather as the beginning of an ongoing relationship with the Spirit of God. Moreover, while testifying before the Sanhedrin (the Jewish religious leaders), Peter exclaims that God gives the Holy Spirit to those who obey Him (Acts 5:32).

In Acts 6:5, a man named Stephen is described as being full of faith and full of the Holy Spirit. In verse 8, he is also described as a man full of God's grace and power who "did great wonders and miraculous signs among the people." Once again, we see a correlation between being full of the Holy Spirit and engaging in supernatural ministry. Later, while he was testifying of Christ before certain religious leaders, Stephen was suddenly filled with the Holy Spirit and supernaturally given sight to look up to heaven and to visibly see the glory of God and Jesus standing at the Father's right hand (Acts 7:55-56).

In the eighth chapter of Acts, Philip preached to the people of Samaria and numerous people chose to believe in Christ. These converts, including a former sorcerer named Simon, were then baptized in water. Shortly thereafter, Peter and John came to Samaria where they prayed for these new believers in Christ to receive the Holy Spirit. Again, we see a scenario in which those who had previously placed faith in the Lord Jesus now receive a subsequent baptism in the Holy Spirit. Although the passage doesn't clearly indicate what immediate effect took place as a result of this outpouring of the Holy Spirit, it does tell us that observing it had instant and dramatic impact on Simon the former sorcerer

— so much so that he offered the disciples money in hopes that they would show him how to lay hands on others with the same result of people receiving the Holy Spirit (a request for which he is sternly rebuked!). There is very little question that the outpouring was immediately observable as producing some sort of significant and immediate outward change.

Acts 9 tells the account of how Saul the Pharisee (who would later become known as the Apostle Paul) was confronted with the sudden reality of Jesus while he was on the way to the city of Damascus to persecute believers. This life-changing encounter radically altered his destiny as he surrendered to the lordship of Christ. Three days later, he was filled with the Holy Spirit when a believer named Ananias placed his hands on him and prayed for him. Interestingly, Saul went on to be baptized in water after this baptism in the Holy Spirit (Acts 9:17-19.)

In Acts 10, Peter preached to the household of Cornelius, a Gentile (non-Jewish) man. As he was speaking, the Holy Spirit was suddenly poured out on all the hearers to the astonishment of the Jewish believers who were present. The text also tells us that Peter and the believers who came with him recognized this as an outpouring of the Spirit because the household of Cornelius were all *"speaking in tongues and praising God"* (Acts 10:44-48). Again, the filling of the Spirit was demonstrably visible, and their submission to the lordship of Christ was made complete through baptism in water after this outpouring of the Spirit. Peter also refers to this outpouring as being what Jesus talked about when He said, *"You will be baptized with the Holy Spirit"* (Acts 11:15-17).

The final account in the book of Acts that deals with the baptism in the Holy Spirit occurs in chapter 19. While ministering in Ephesus, Paul encountered people who had repented of their sins but apparently had not yet submitted to the lordship of Jesus. They had not even heard about the Holy Spirit. After they opened their hearts to believe in Jesus, Paul then laid his hands on them, and they were saturated with the Holy Spirit and began speaking in tongues and prophesying.

THE IMPACT OF SPIRIT BAPTISM

Having reviewed these various passages from Acts, it is significant to realize that in every single account of people being initially baptized in the Holy Spirit, there is also an immediate, demonstrative, observable impact. Sometimes the baptism happens as people are praying, sometimes through the laying on of hands, and sometimes as people hear the Gospel and choose to believe. With the lone exception of Acts 10, it is otherwise apparent that the baptism in the Spirit is generally a subsequent event following the acceptance of Christ as Lord. Yet, it could also be easily argued in the case of Cornelius's household that while the people may have technically believed first, and only then were baptized in the Holy Spirit, the reality is that these actions happened in such rapid, fluid succession as to be essentially experienced simultaneously. It also seems important to note that after having been initially saturated with the Spirit, believers continued to experience subsequent "fillings." As the book of Acts progresses, it becomes especially apparent that this Holy Spirit baptism has enabled believers to continue in an ongoing, interactive relationship with the Spirit of God (Acts 5:32; 8:29, 39; 9:31; 10:19; 11:12, 28; 13:2, 4; 15:28; 16:6-7; 20:22-23; 21:4, 11).

Some today might ask if God intends for people to still be baptized in the Spirit with similar resulting empowerment and Christlike character. There is absolutely nothing in the Scriptures to indicate that this is not the case. In fact, there are numerous biblical writings which would be effectively rendered irrelevant and useless if we were to argue that the baptism in the Holy Spirit or its subsequent supernatural enablement were no longer meant to take place. Why would we follow the biblical injunctions to pray for the sick (James 5:13-15) if there were no reason to believe God wants to minister in gifts of healing by the Spirit (1 Corinthians 12:9)? Jesus told His disciples in Acts 1:8 that they would receive power to be His witnesses when the Holy Spirit came upon them. Surely, He still desires that His followers would be empowered witnesses today! Paul tells the church to eagerly desire spiritual gifts and to try to excel in gifts that build up the church (1 Corinthians 14:1,12). How can we follow this instruction unless the baptism in the Spirit is still taking place? In this way, the Bible makes it obvious that this baptism and continual filling is meant to be the experience of believers even now.

RECEIVING THE BAPTISM OF THE HOLY SPIRIT

How does this baptism in the Holy Spirit actually occur? We should note that the Scripture is not formulaic in its approach; it does not outline a single, step-by-step process. As an obvious starting point, though, the Scripture does point first to submitting to the lordship of Jesus Christ. There is no point or opportunity to receive the baptism in the Holy Spirit if we have not embraced Jesus as our Lord and Savior.

Additionally of note, on more than one occasion the Holy Spirit was poured out when another believer laid hands on and prayed for the recipient. Though this is certainly not seen as an absolute or the only way to be baptized with the Spirit, it is commonly described. Most important, though, in Luke 11:13 (NLT) Jesus says the Father gives the Holy Spirit to those who ask. In verses 9-10 of that passage, Jesus tells us how to ask for anything from God. *"And so I tell you, keep on asking, and you will receive what you ask for. Keep on seeking, and you will find. Keep on knocking, and the door will be opened to you. For everyone who asks, receives. Everyone who seeks, finds. And to everyone who knocks, the door will be opened."* These verses show us the importance of an expectant and persistent mindset when we pray. In Acts 1, we find a demonstration of this principle. The text tells us that once the followers of Jesus understood that God wanted to give them this new experience, this baptism in the Spirit, they didn't leave Jerusalem and go their separate ways, but instead joined together and devoted themselves to seeking the Father and praying for this gift until it was received (Acts 1:13-14). For them, it took ten days!

Jesus told us that when we pray, we should believe that we have already received from Him, even while we are asking (Mark 11:24). Based on this principle, here is one possible outline for receiving the baptism in the Holy Spirit. You can follow these steps on your own or even get together with another Spirit-filled believer and ask them to lay hands on you and pray.

1. Understand that we must first give our lives over to Jesus. Confess Him as your Lord and Savior, turn from your sins, trust in His grace, and devote yourself completely to Him.
2. Understand that Jesus wants to baptize us with the Holy Spirit in order to fill us with Christlike character and to give us power to be witnesses for Him in this world.
3. Ask the Lord Jesus to baptize you in the Holy Spirit.
4. Choose to believe and receive by faith this promised gift of God.
5. Expect both immediate and ongoing, long-term transformation.

6. Anticipate that the Lord will distribute spiritual gifts as He chooses and that any of them could begin to take place in the moment. Speaking in tongues is a common occurrence.
7. Expect and seek additional spiritual gifts and other biblical manifestations of the Spirit's presence and power.

POSSIBLE ASSUMPTIONS AND CORRECTIONS

Steps four and five are where many people stumble in this process. Some falsely assume that if they don't have some incredible and/or emotional experience that somehow, they have not therefore been baptized in the Spirit, but the Bible doesn't say that. It says the Lord gives the Holy Spirit to those who ask. Period. Having prayed in accordance with that promise, then, it is good and right to expect certain things to happen.

Throughout the book of Acts, in almost every instance where people received the Holy Spirit, they also spoke in tongues (and when it is not specifically mentioned, it may be inferred). This means they spoke in words and syllables that they didn't necessarily understand. Let's be careful not to be confused by that statement. Nothing took over their lips and vocal chords or forced their mouths to emit strange sounds. Rather, the Spirit provided the words and they chose to speak them out. Experientially, some people say they first "hear" these words "inside"; others "feel" them. It's a spiritual experience that is hard to describe and may vary from person to person in how it manifests. The Bible says that when we speak in tongues, we declare mysteries with our spirit back to God. Doing so builds us up and adds strength to our lives (1 Corinthians 14:2-4; Jude 20). In accordance with this, many believers around the world practice a "private prayer language" as part of an experience of private devotion before the Lord through which they experience a strengthening from God. Speaking in tongues is not a necessary and required "proof" of being baptized in the Spirit, but it is a common experience for many and often observed in the biblical examples of Spirit-infilling. Additionally, any of the spiritual gifts can certainly take place, and all of them should be sought, especially those that build up the church.

Sometimes if people don't initially speak in tongues, they can make one of at least two false assumptions. First, they may think, "Well, I must not be baptized in the Spirit after all." This is a wrong assumption because receiving the Spirit is a matter of faith, not a matter of a certain type of outward experience. Second, they may think, "I am baptized in the Spirit, but apparently God doesn't want me to speak in tongues." Tongues is *not* the *determining* factor in receiving the Spirit, but it very likely could be an *eventual* one in the same way that all of the spiritual gifts are to be sought out and anticipated. This doesn't mean that every Spirit baptized believer will actually display every possible spiritual gift, but it does mean that the Spirit certainly could work any of His gifts in us as He desires. None of us should shut the door on any spiritual gift thinking, "That one is not for me." In 1 Corinthians 14:5, Paul wished that every single one of us would speak in tongues and even more that we would prophesy!

Finally, just because someone has been baptized in the Spirit doesn't mean that they should not also practice a disciplined prayer life or regular time with the Lord. To be baptized means to be immersed in the Spirit. But even as a soaked sponge can dry out over time unless re-submerged in water, so too we must be regularly and continually filled with the Holy Spirit. Paul writes in Ephesians 5:18, *"Do not get drunk on wine, which leads to debauchery. Instead, be filled with the Spirit."* The phrase "be filled" uses a verb tense in the original language which literally means "be being filled," or "continually be filled with the Spirit." The Lord wants our lives to be a portrait of the life and ministry of Jesus. We need to be saturated with the Holy Spirit just as He was. Also, like Jesus, we can create opportunity to be continually filled with the Spirit by deciding to spend regular time in the Father's presence.

OPENING TO SPIRIT BAPTISM

If you are looking for a place to start, here's a prayer that you can offer. It's not necessary, of course, to use these exact words. It is, however, about being authentic with the Lord and coming to Him in simple faith. Find a place and time where you can get before the Lord without distractions. You may want to sit on a chair or even lie down on the floor. Visualize yourself coming to Jesus as you bring to Him a prayer that could go something like this, but in your own words:

> **Heavenly Father, I thank You that You are my Lord. I have trusted in Your work on the cross and You have saved me from my sins. Thanks for transforming my life and bringing me into**

Your Kingdom. I now believe that You want to baptize me with Your Holy Spirit so that I can be an effective witness for You. Lord, I need Your character, Your fruit growing in my life. I desire for You to pour out supernatural gifts and miracles through my life so that others can be brought closer to You. So I ask you right now to baptize me, to fill me, to saturate me with Your Holy Spirit. Bring Your cleansing, Your passion, Your heart, and Your power. Thank You, Lord! I receive by faith the gift of Your Holy Spirit right now. All of this I pray and ask in the name of Jesus. Amen.

Having prayed this prayer, expect God to answer and have faith that He is doing so right now. You may want to focus on His love for you and to meditate on His goodness toward you. Allow Him to saturate you with His Spirit. You may feel the dramatic sense of the Spirit overwhelming you, or you may experience the quiet rest and peace He often brings. On the other hand, it is also entirely possible that you may not feel any kind of emotional response. No matter what, trust that your Heavenly Father, who loves giving good gifts to His children, is pouring out His Holy Spirit on you just as He promised He would.

It is also a common experience that people will begin to speak in tongues as they are filled with the Spirit. So if (or when) you begin to "sense" funny syllables that you don't understand, choose to speak them. Continue for as long as you feel that freedom. Your spirit is speaking mysteries to God, and you will discover strength flowing into your life.

PERSONAL STORIES CAN VARY

Spirit baptism doesn't necessarily look or happen the same way with every recipient. In my case, I gave my heart to Christ at an early age. By the time I was thirteen years old, I had been taught about the baptism in the Holy Spirit and wanted to enter into this new experience. However, I was completely intimidated about going to the altar in front of everyone to receive prayer. After a few weeks of wrestling with this dilemma, I made a decision to ask the Lord to baptize me. I didn't go to the altar at the front of the church. I simply offered the Lord my own prayer while our congregation was engaged in a time of extended praise and worship. Immediately I felt the Lord's presence surround me, and I began to hear the beginnings of a language I did not know inside my mind. It was just a few starting phrases. As I chose to speak them forth, those phrases turned into many as I found myself speaking in tongues. I was overwhelmed with a new sense of Spirit empowerment. In the weeks and months that followed, I had a renewed hunger for both personal holiness and for sharing Christ with others. My life began to change as I began to live in recognition and cooperation with the Spirit of God.

My mother's story was a bit different. She had learned about the baptism in the Holy Spirit through the charismatic renewal movement that swept through the denominational churches during the 1970s. She had become involved with a women's Bible study that was intent on discovering more about the ways of the Spirit. That group of ladies had all laid hands on my mom and prayed that she would be baptized in the Spirit. She later said she felt the Lord's presence as an overwhelming peace but didn't find herself speaking in tongues. Nevertheless, she thanked the Lord for filling her with His Spirit. Sometime long after that, she was standing in her kitchen washing dishes. As she worked along, she began singing praise songs to the Lord. She started by singing familiar choruses and then transitioned to singing spontaneous words from her heart as she worshiped the Lord. She did this for a while when suddenly, to her great surprise, she realized she was no longer using English but was singing in tongues! The discovery so startled her that she immediately stopped and touched her hand to her lips . . . only to find that she had subsequently covered them with the suds from the sink as she was still doing the dishes! Other than finding this hilarious, I think it is notable that she wasn't necessarily focused on seeking "tongues" (though she was still trusting God that it would eventually happen) but rather simply giving praise and adoration to God. In the midst of her heartfelt worship, the Lord began to manifest the gift of speaking in tongues. The baptism in the Holy Spirit had already taken place!

A third account involves an older woman who was part of a congregation where I once served as pastor. She had become quite frustrated that she had never spoken in tongues despite receiving prayer multiple times over many decades. For her, Spirit baptism had become synonymous with speaking in tongues, and she was quite disillusioned, thinking that the Lord was somehow unwilling to baptize her in the Spirit. As I ministered to her, I let her know that speaking in tongues is an evidence of Spirit baptism, but certainly not the only evidence. She was a woman of noble character and deep devotion to the Lord. I assured her that the fruit of the Spirit was amply seen in her life and that other gifts were also apparent. Secondly, I presented her with the truth that the Spirit of God was not going to take over her lips and make her speak in tongues. If she was waiting for this to happen, it would be likely that she would continue to wait. Rather, I encouraged her to relax and simply choose to open her mouth and speak if and when she in any way simply had a sense of unknown words inside of her. I prayed for the peace of God to fill her and for all humanly induced pressure to "perform" to leave. Within seconds, she began to speak in tongues, and her face lit up in joyful delight. She later remarked that she had felt words of this nature for a long time but thought some force was supposed to take over. What a relief it was for her to realize the Spirit wanted to work in cooperation with her and that she only needed to yield to Him.

In addition to these stories, I have also met many kinds of people who fully love the Lord and who have clearly demonstrated the fruit of the Spirit actively through their lives. In addition to the spiritual gifts of 1 Corinthians 12, other Spirit-empowered gifts such as those found in Romans 12 are quite evident (serving, teaching, encouraging, leadership, mercy, and others), but these individuals have never spoken in tongues. They are no less filled with the Spirit than others, but simply manifest different gifts. Spiritual gifts are not to be used as some kind of spiritual litmus test or as a means of comparing ourselves one to another. By no means! May we be zealous for every spiritual gift and then follow the way of love at all times as we appreciate the Spirit's unique work in one another.

LIVING YOUR OWN STORY

If you have asked the Lord Jesus to baptize you in the Holy Spirit, then trust and believe by faith that you have the Holy Spirit. Now choose to regularly draw near to the Lord in prayer, asking Him to continually fill you. You will be amazed at the transformation that begins to overtake your life. The Holy Spirit is sent to us to be a helper and to work on our behalf. Jesus said in John 14:16-17, *"I will ask the Father, and he will give you another Counselor to be with you forever — the Spirit of truth. The world cannot accept him, because it neither sees him nor knows him. But you know him, for he lives with you and will be*

> **PAUSE AND REFLECT:**
>
> - How does this chapter reflect your previous understanding of the baptism in the Holy Spirit? What is the same? What has been challenged? What has encouraged you?
>
> - What has been your experience of receiving the baptism in the Holy Spirit? What have you observed in others? What have you experienced yourself?
>
> - What misconceptions or misunderstandings about Spirit baptism have you had? What questions still remain?
>
> - What is your next step in experiencing the baptism in the Holy Spirit and living a Spirit-filled life? Who could you connect with to help answer questions and explore further?

in you." The result of Spirit baptism is that the Holy Spirit indwells us and saturates us with His presence and power. His love for us is the same regardless of whether we've experienced the baptism in the Holy Spirit or not, but His hope is that we might all trust Him to fill us in this way. Let's not be afraid to reach out to Him today. He really loves us and wants to fill us to overflowing with Himself.

Chapter 3
The Spirit Working in Us

Psalm 1 gives us a wonderful picture of an individual who has been blessed by God. This opening Psalm describes someone who refuses to walk in step with the wicked and who will not embrace the lifestyle and attitude of those steeped in sin. Instead, this person finds delight in the law of God and then chooses to meditate on His ways day and night. The author provides an analogy to help us understand how the Lord sees such a person. The psalmist writes, *"He is like a tree planted by streams of water, which yields its fruit in season and whose leaf does not wither. Whatever he does prospers"* (Psalm 1:3). The image is vibrant and robust. We can easily see this tree in our mind's eye, drawing nutrients from the continual flow of water next to it and producing wholesome, desirable fruit. We continue to see the illustration of finding life in flowing water in the New Testament as well.

LIVING WATER

The Gospel of John makes reference to "living water." The idea of living water is that it is water on the move, water that flows. A pond is still water. A stream is living water. A well is still water. A spring is living water. In Israel, the Sea of Galilee continually receives a fresh flow of water. It's fed from the north by the Jordan River. At the southern end, the river continues. Because of this, there is a constant and regular sense of renewal because the water is regularly replenished. As a result, the Sea of Galilee is full of life, hosting multiple species of fish. Numerous communities dot the shoreline. For thousands of years, people have found the resources they have needed to survive and thrive through the living water that is found in the Sea of Galilee.

As the Jordan River reforms at the base of the Sea of Galilee, it travels south and eventually spills into the Dead Sea. Here the conditions are quite different. The Dead Sea has no outlet. The same water that flows in and out of the Sea of Galilee flows into this second lake, but it has no place to go. In the hot and harsh conditions of that region, the water stagnates and evaporates, leaving behind massive amounts of salt. The result is that nothing can live in the Dead Sea. There are no fish within its waters. There is no vegetation below the surface. What's the difference? The water in the Sea of Galilee is continually moving, flowing, and replenishing. It is living water, but the water of the Dead Sea simply collects and becomes lifeless.

The Psalm 1 passage pictures for us a person who has become fruitful and full of life because they have been planted next to living water. In John 7:38, Jesus says, *"Whoever believes in me . . . streams of living water will flow from within him."* To make sure that the reader is not confused, John clarifies, *"By this he meant the Spirit, whom those who believed in him were later to receive"* (John 7:39). God's intent is to fill us all with a continual flow of the Holy Spirit in order to make us just like the tree of that first Psalm — fruitful, strong, prosperous, and full of life.

The living water of the Spirit flowing into and through the life of a believer brings significant impact in two major ways. First, there are the internal workings of the Spirit. In other words, the presence and power of the Holy Spirit begins to shape and give rise to Christlike qualities that grow and develop in each person who looks to Christ as Lord. The book of Galatians calls these qualities the fruit of the Spirit. They are produced by the living water of the Spirit as it flows within us. Second, there are the external workings of the Spirit, when the Spirit produces abilities and actions that come through our lives in powerful and dramatic ways to bring change and life to those around us, sometimes in dramatic ways. Paul's letters refer to these as *gifts* of the Spirit.

Both the fruit and the gifts of the Spirit are evidences of His presence flowing in and through the Spirit. They are meant to work together to touch others in ways that will draw them to the Lord as well. As we are filled with the Spirit, we become a wellspring of living water that is meant to nurture the people whom God places in our sphere of influence. Through Christlike character and supernatural power that comes from the Spirit of God, the lives of those around us can be encouraged, strengthened, and directed to the lordship of Jesus. Let's embrace a brief scriptural overview of these internal and external workings of the Spirit.

THE FRUIT OF THE SPIRIT

In the fifth chapter of his letter to the Galatians, the Apostle Paul instructs the church to turn from various sins and outworkings of their fleshly desires by choosing to walk in step with the Holy Spirit. He then writes that *"the fruit of the Spirit is love, joy, peace, patience, kindness, goodness, faithfulness, gentleness and self-control"* (Galatians 5:22-23). In other words, as we open our hearts to live by the Spirit, we can expect that He will produce in us these character qualities as He conforms us more and more into the image of Christ. That is, after all, the Father's intent for each of us. In Romans 8:29, Paul also writes, *"For those God foreknew, he also predestined to be conformed to the image of His Son."* By his Spirit, the Lord is rearranging our hearts and working to make us look like Jesus. That's why the Scripture indicates that these Christlike virtues are fruit that comes from the Holy Spirit. They are not the product of our human nature, but they are instead meant to grow in us by the lifegiving stream of the Spirit's living water. They are not the product of our effort and work, but rather the organic outgrowth of the Spirit of God within us. That doesn't mean that we are supposed to be passive, to just sit back and wait for this fruit to emerge. Not at all! Rather, we are to yield to and cooperate with what the Spirit is doing as He works to produce this fruit within us. As others begin to see and taste of this fruit, God's intent is that they will get a taste of Him! Psalm 34:8 declares, *"Taste and see that the Lord is good."* The Holy Spirit produces fruit on the inside of us that transforms us from the inside out and offers something lasting to those around us. This process is part of the internal workings of the Spirit. Consider what is meant by each of the nine fruits of the Spirit presented by Paul.

The first one listed is *love*, and there is a sense as we read the passage that all the rest of the fruits of the Spirit are ways of demonstrating and extending this essential quality. Love is the foundation of all the Scripture. When asked which commandment in all of the Law was the greatest, Jesus responded, *"'Love the Lord your God with all your heart and with all your soul and with all your mind.' This is the first and greatest commandment. And the second is like it: 'Love your neighbor as yourself.' All the Law and the Prophets hang on these two commandments"* (Matthew 22:37-40). Where there is love, there is motivation to honor and obey God. When love is evident, so is the desire to serve and care for people. Love chooses to value people regardless of their past or present actions. This kind of love is not conditional upon someone else's conduct or performance. It is a sacrificial love that esteems others as the creation of our Heavenly Father. It is the kind of love that Christ Jesus has for all of us. It is the kind of love He wants to extend to others through us.

Where love is prioritized, *joy* naturally follows. Joy is not merely the feeling of happiness that stems from circumstances and events transpiring around us in a delightful way. It is also the internal fire of hope that has learned to rejoice in the Lord even when facing adversity, hardship, and pain. We can confront even the worst of circumstances with a joy that springs up from the reservoir of the Spirit within us. At all times, we can be assured of the love of God — and if He loves us, no matter what, there is ample reason to be truly joyful.

Third on the list of spiritual fruit is *peace*. This peace includes not only a sense of inner contentment and tranquility, but also the ability to influence reconciliation and unity. As the Lord's peace grows within us, we can let go of our human propensity to argue and fight with others. Even more, we can become instruments of the Lord's peace and offer an invitation for others to find calmness. Where there is right relationship with God as found in Christ, there is an opportunity to receive and to give away peace. Again, it comes from the Spirit of the Lord within us. It is notable that four of the five writings of John, as well as both letters by Peter and every epistle written by Paul, include a blessing of peace to others. The Lord is looking to impart peace by His Spirit!

The New International Version (1884) of this Scripture next lists *patience*. The King James Bible prefers the word *longsuffering*. The idea is almost intimidating. Who wants to suffer for a long time? Moreover, how is this a virtue of the Spirit? Yet the word means so much more than what we might first realize. It includes the ability to persevere, no matter how difficult the trial. It represents the grace to calmly endure while trusting that God's goodness is greater than the hardship of any circumstance. We can hold back from fear or despair because we know that we are divinely loved. Because we are allowing the Lord's love to overflow through us, we can hold back our anger and the aggression that want to strike back at those who sin against us. We can instead put up with the failings and shortcomings of others and choose to be gracious.

Where there is *kindness*, there is thoughtfulness and generosity. This is also evidence of a loving heart. *Goodness* includes the pursuit of all that is ethical and right. It looks to serve the interests of others before the interests of self. *Faithfulness* is sometimes simply translated as *faith*. As this fruit of the Spirit develops, trustworthiness grows. So does an enduring trust in God as an ever-deepening hope and confidence in His Word take root in us. What the NIV translates as *gentleness* is also often translated as "meekness" or "humility." It is the ability to respond to others with "considerateness," even when we are not treated in the same way. When we exhibit this fruit, there is no need to defend ourselves, to show how strong we think we are, or to prove ourselves right in front of others. Instead, we can choose to act from a place of mercy and compassion.

This list of Spirit-produced fruit ends with *self-control.* This peace includes the ability to say "no!" to the temptations and influence of sin. Instead of giving in to fleshly lusts and desires, responding to others in angry and inappropriate ways, or pursuing vices and habits that only bring destruction, we can choose to honor God. Titus 2:11 declares, *"For the grace of God that brings salvation has appeared to all men. It teaches us to say 'No' to ungodliness and worldly passions, and to live self-controlled, upright and godly lives in this present age."* This grace from God is divine power by the Spirit.

As we are filled with His streams of living water, His fruit grows all the more, and we are empowered to turn from sinful ways and to instead pursue acts of righteousness that touch the world with the kingdom of God. In this way, what the Spirit produces on the *inside* of us begins to manifest in supernatural ways on the *outside* of us. With that in mind, let's consider a brief overview of the external workings of the Spirit. His supernatural gifts are meant to manifest through us and bring aid to others in ways that are practical (and sometimes dramatic) in order to help people see and experience the goodness of God for themselves.

THE GIFTS OF THE SPIRIT

Most of us realize that the Bible wasn't written in English. The Old Testament was originally and predominately written in Hebrew, while the New Testament was written originally in Greek. When it comes to the discussion of spiritual gifts, what we may not realize is that the Greek Scriptures use a variety of different terms that all get translated into English as "gifts" or "spiritual gifts." When Paul wrote his first letter to the church in Corinth, he devoted a large portion of chapters 12, 13, and 14 to the discussion of spiritual gifts. A short exploration of his use of various Greek terms can help us understand the purpose and intent that God has for pouring out spiritual gifts through us by His Spirit.

The Greek word for "Spirit" is *pneuma*. Back in chapter 1, we mentioned that depending on the context, this word is also used to indicate "breath" or even "wind," especially when understood as coming from God. As Paul launches into chapter 12 of 1 Corinthians, it is interesting to note that he writes, *"Now about the **gifts of the Spirit**, brothers, I do not want you to be ignorant"* (verse 1). The phrase "gifts of the Spirit" comes from a single Greek word: *pneumatikon*. We can see the root word, *pneuma*, right there in the front portion. Paul is conveying that there are displays of power that come through the Church as gifts that are enabled by the Spirit of God. As the chapter unfolds, Paul will use a series of different but similar words to help us understand the nature of these spiritual gifts.

In verse 4, he continues, *"There are different kinds of gifts, but the same Spirit."* In English, we simply see a repeat of the word "gifts," but in the original Greek language, the text uses a different word altogether: *charismaton*. It means "gifts empowered by grace." Paul is not changing subjects by using this new term but is instead helping us to understand what spiritual gifts are by using a similar word. These gifts are not simply human talents or abilities. They are examples of divine enablement produced directly by the Holy Spirit within us. They are demonstrations of His ability, not ours. It is the Spirit of God who distributes these gifts to us as an outgrowth of His presence within us. As Paul continues, more information comes to light. *"There are different kinds of service, but the same Lord"* (verse 5). This means that there are lots of different ways of doing ministry through which the gifts of the Spirit can be utilized to help others. He says, *"There are different kinds of working"* (verse 6). That is to say that there are many different kinds of results and impacts that these gifts can produce, *"but the same God works all of them in all men"* (verse 6). In other] words, there are no absolute set rules for how these spiritual gifts must necessarily show up and work, but when they do, all glory and honor is meant to go to the Lord, not to us. The gifts belong to Him; we just have the privilege and opportunity to become a conduit for the presence and power of the Spirit.

Verse 7 shows us the purpose for these spiritual gifts: *"Now to each one the manifestation of the Spirit is given for the common good."* The presence and power of the Spirit is made visible in order to bring together a real sense of aid and help for everyone. The Holy Spirit is here to assist us in a tangible way and to work through us to bring real practical benefit to others. In John 14:16-17, the New American Standard Bible records that Jesus told his disciples, *"I will ask the Father, and He will give you another Helper, so that he may be with you forever; the Helper is the Spirit of truth."* The Holy Spirit helps us in our weakness. He releases spiritual gifts to provide those in need with an experience of God's favor, blessing, and divine assistance. This is the intent for each of the spiritual gifts that Paul is about to describe.

In 1 Corinthians 12:8-10, Paul lists nine supernatural gifts. These include 1) a message of wisdom (the ability to divinely know and share what to do and how to act), 2) a message of knowledge (being aware of events or information solely by means of the Spirit), 3) faith (a sudden empowerment to trust God and act on His Word), 4) gifts of healing (the divine ability to address and rectify a variety of illnesses and infirmities), 5) miraculous powers (the release of divine energy that defies and overcomes the apparent laws of nature), 6) prophecy (the ability to convey and make clear the heart, mind, and words of God in specific settings and circumstances), 7) distinguishing between spirits (being able to make right judgments and to distinguish what is of God and what is not), 8) speaking in different kinds of tongues (the enablement to speak in unknown languages and/or divine ecstatic speech), and 9) the interpretation of tongues (the sharing of the meaning and intent of what has been first presented via speaking in tongues).

Displays of this kind of spiritual activity are not meant to be signs of someone's spirituality, insight, or personal connection with God. Rather, these gifts are moves of the Spirit in response to those in need. They are given for the common good, for our mutual benefit. Such gifts come about in accordance with the distribution and will of the Holy Spirit as He sees fit. Implicit in calling them "gifts of the Spirit" is the understanding that they cannot be earned. They are not rewards for good behavior. They are gifts of God, empowerments of the Spirit that bring practical, tangible, experiential help to others in some way as the Spirit works to draw people to Christ and deepen their relationship with Him. Having said that, this does not mean that these spiritual gifts are haphazard or arbitrary. We can grow in our development, experience, and deployment of these gifts. We've already read in 1 Corinthians 12:1 that Paul wants to be sure that we are informed about these gifts. In verses 28-31 of this chapter, we are also told that not all of us will individually manifest each and every single one of these gifts, but that we should all desire the greater gifts — those displays of the Spirit that will bring about the most good as needed. There certainly seems to be a connection, then, between desiring the good of those around us and seeing spiritual gifts manifest in our lives. For that to happen, it is important that our churches become intentional about fostering an expectation and environment for spiritual gifts to manifest and develop. Such manifestations are gifts operated and conducted by the Spirit, but we can certainly become better adept at listening to the Spirit and allowing Him to work through us. The Spirit certainly wants to make Himself known in this way. He is looking to touch people's lives in powerful ways, and He wants to work through each of us. Why else would He call us to eagerly desire such gifts?

Some believers and some churches get nervous about the pursuit of spiritual gifts. Indeed, some people have sought them with wrong motives, and others have allowed them to become a source of spiritual pride. This can lead to destructive patterns when left unchecked. But the correction of the improper use of anything, including spiritual gifts, is not to end their use, but rather to seek out proper, Spirit-led and Christ-honoring use. Paul addresses spiritual gifts in his letter to Corinth not to shut down spiritual gifts, but instead to help them be deployed properly. In fact, in Part 2 of this book, we will examine options and considerations for how churches can begin to establish a framework to better ensure that spiritual gifts and the workings of the Spirit are pursued and explored in a healthy way.

1 Corinthians is not the only place in Scripture where spiritual gifts are mentioned. In Romans 12:6, Paul also writes, *"We have different gifts ("charismata" – the same word as used in 1 Corinthians), according to the grace given to each of us."* The descriptions that follow in this passage are sometimes referred to as "motivational gifts." Beyond momentary displays of the Spirit's power, these gifts seem to convey ongoing actions and activities in the life of the church: prophesying, serving, teaching, encouraging, generous giving, leading, and showing mercy (Romans 12:6-8). Moreover, in Ephesians 4:7-8, Paul makes reference to when Christ ascended into heaven and asserts that as He rose, by His grace He "gave gifts to men." Here, "gifts" is another Greek word altogether (domata). It is typically a word used to describe a tangible, physical present. Paul writes that among these tangible gifts given to the people are those of apostles, prophets, evangelists, and pastors/teachers (Ephesians 4:11). Clearly, across a variety of ways, the Spirit is working to empower the Church in order to achieve a beneficial impact on the rest of society.

With these various depictions of spiritual gifts in action, I would like to suggest that none of these apparent lists are necessarily meant to be complete. Rather, it seems they are but a sampling of the kind of things the Spirit can and will do as He works in the lives of people. We've already read that there are many different kinds of service and many different kinds of working with spiritual gifts (1 Corinthians 12:5-6). In addition, Jesus told his disciples in John 14:12, *I tell you the truth, anyone who has faith in me will do what I have been doing. He will do even greater things than these, because I am going to the Father."* He goes on to say that as He returns to the Father, the Father will then send them the Spirit! There is no limit to what the Spirit can and will do through the lives of those who believe. Jesus emphatically declared, *"You may ask me for anything in my name, and I will do it!"* (John 14:14). The lists of spiritual gifts found in the Scripture may be just the beginnings of what the Spirit would like to do as He works to bring people into the kingdom of God. Whatever gifts or other workings of the Spirit that may manifest should demonstrate God's love, serve to meet the needs of others, and point people back to the lordship of Jesus. The emphasis will always be on message and the ministry, but not on the exaltation of the human messenger or minister. Where supernatural workings of the Spirit truly occur, the fruit of the Spirit will be made apparent as well.

WE NEED THEM BOTH

The fruit and the gifts of the Spirit are both important aspects of the flow of the Spirit in our lives. In fact, I'd like to suggest that one is foundational to the other. As the fruit of the Spirit develops in our lives, we become people of Christlike character, centered first and foremost in the love of God. Then as spiritual gifts begin to manifest, they become directed and guided by the virtues of the Spirit that have grown on the inside of us. The internal and external workings of the Spirit are both meant to flourish in us. This is how a life in the Spirit is supposed to look. However, sometimes we can be prone to pursue only one aspect and fail to fully see the value in the other. This leads to a lopsided, ineffective Christian faith.

When we ignore the gifts of the Spirit, when we falsely believe that they are not meant for us today or that God would never use us in that way, we make a tremendous error. If we focus only on the development of the fruit of the Spirit in our lives, we may indeed grow in the love and goodness of Christ, but when it comes to being used by God to meet needs as they arise around us, our impact may be limited. Our ability to help will go only as far as our own talent, skill, and creativity can take us. It doesn't take long for any of us to discover that the issues and obstacles of life are bigger than we are. We need the presence and power of the Holy Spirit. If we are unable to trust Him to flow through us in supernatural ways, we will fall short of the hopes and intentions of God as He looks to touch the world with His goodness and to draw people everywhere to Himself. Conversely, if we become zealous for spiritual gifts without growing in character and maturity through the fruit of the Spirit, we also err, and we will surely end up bringing reproach upon both ourselves and our Lord. We are all acquainted with numerous people, both locally and in the broader Church, who have had powerful ministries that seemed to touch a lot of people only to be subsequently brought down by hidden sins, pride, and abusive relationships. Such corruption always has detrimental impact far greater than one might anticipate. How many of us know someone who has turned their back on the Lord and fallen away from their faith in Christ because of character issues that became apparent in someone who otherwise seemed to be anointed and empowered by God in supernatural ways? It is not enough to have one or the other. We need to actively invite and pursue the development of both the fruit of the Spirit and the gifts of the Spirit.

In chapter 5, we will begin to explore various foundations and guidelines that churches may want to consider as they purpose to help their congregations become well-rounded disciples of Jesus, marked by both fruitful, godly character and manifestations of spiritual gifts that make a real difference in the lives of others. Before we get there, though, let's take a moment to address an aspect of Spirit-filled living that tends to be a stumbling block for many Christ-followers: What's the fuss about speaking in tongues? Is this still an important aspect of life in the Spirit? What if you've never experienced this gift of the Spirit? What does the Bible have to say about it? Let's take a moment to zero in on these questions in the next chapter.

> **PAUSE AND REFLECT:**
>
> As you consider the flow of the Holy Spirit's living water in your own life, do you feel more like the Sea of Galilee or the Dead Sea? If there are areas of your spiritual life that have grown stagnant, what steps can you take to invite the Spirit to stir the waters again?
>
> As you reflect on the fruit of the Spirit, where have you experienced the most growth? What might be the next area that the Spirit would like to emphasize as He works to make you even more fruitful?
>
> In what ways has the Lord used spiritual gifts in your life? What gifts do you desire for Him to work through you? Why? What is your motivation?
>
> As you consider how both the fruit of the Spirit and the gifts of the Spirit are being demonstrated in and through you, would you say you are pretty much balanced ... or lopsided? How can you deliberately seek the Lord to address areas that may need greater emphasis?

Chapter 4
Speaking in Tongues

In 1 Corinthians 14:5, the Apostle Paul under the inspiration of the Holy Spirit writes, *"I would like every one of you to speak in tongues . . . ."* Yet, many Christians today are confused and even scared by the idea of speaking in tongues. Some think that it is a gift that is no longer present in the Church. Others may have come to an altar and prayed to receive it but not having experienced the gift so far have concluded that "tongues" must not be for them. Still others suggest that if a person does not speak in tongues, they don't really have the Holy Spirit. A select minority would even argue that one can't go to heaven without first speaking in tongues. So, what is the truth about speaking in tongues? What is it really? What purpose does it serve? Who is it for? Is this really meant to be part of the life of the believer today? How do people speak in tongues? Let's attempt to explore these questions by looking at what the Scriptures have to say.

TONGUES IN THE GOSPELS

The gift of tongues is first mentioned in Mark 16:17. There Jesus says, *". . . these signs will accompany those who believe: In my name they will drive out demons; they will speak in new tongues."* The word translated "tongues" can also be translated as "language" or "speech." What's interesting about Jesus' description is that He calls them *new* tongues, not merely other tongues or *different* tongues. Could it mean a language never heard before? Possibly and very likely, but we don't have enough information in this passage to say so authoritatively. Nevertheless, the particular word choice is interesting. Also of note is the implication that this experience of tongues is supposed to be one of the signs that can identify a believer in Jesus.

TONGUES ON THE DAY OF PENTECOST

In Acts 2, 120 followers of Jesus had been meeting for prayer for ten continuous days in anticipation of receiving the promised gift from the Father. The gift was the Holy Spirit. As they were seeking the Lord, suddenly a sound like a violent wind filled the room and something that resembled tongues of fire settled over each one. As a result, Acts 2:4 (NIV) says, *"All of them were filled with the Holy Spirit and began to speak in other tongues as the Spirit enabled them."*

There is a definite connection between the infilling of the Holy Spirit and the release of the gift of tongues in this instance. Why were they speaking in tongues? The Bible doesn't address this question in this story. It does not give us a "why"; it just informs us that it happened. It does tell us that as the crowd came to investigate the sound (whether the sound of the tongues or the sound of the rushing wind, we do not know for sure – perhaps both), they each heard the disciples speaking in their own language, declaring the wonders of God.

> ***Now there were staying in Jerusalem God-fearing Jews from every nation under heaven. When they heard this sound, a crowd came together in bewilderment, because each one heard them speaking in his own language. Utterly amazed, they asked: "Are not all these men who are speaking Galileans? Then how is it that each of us hears them in his own native language? Parthians, Medes and Elamites; residents of Mesopotamia, Judea and Cappadocia, Pontus and Asia, Phrygia and Pamphylia, Egypt and the parts of Libya near Cyrene; visitors from Rome (both Jews and converts to Judaism); Cretans and Arabs – we hear them declaring the wonders of God in our own tongues!" (Acts 2:5-11).***

Perhaps this is a double miracle. Those who had gathered in the upper room were speaking in tongues that they did not know, and each person who came to witness this event was hearing their own particular language and dialect. We understand that this could be a double miracle in that exact moment because in later discussions of the gift of tongues (see the Apostle Paul's description in 1 Corinthians 14), it is noted that typically others do not understand when someone speaks in tongues. In fact, the gift of tongues is typically not a language directed to people at all! *"For anyone who speaks in a tongue does not speak to men, but to God"* (1 Corinthians 14:2). Rather, when people speak in tongues they are supposed to pray to be able to interpret so that they and others might understand what is being said. *"Anyone who speaks in a tongue should pray that he may interpret what he says"* (1 Corinthians 14:13). Of course, it is also possible that the tongues being spoken on that particular day were a supernatural release of other known languages since people from all the surrounding nations had come to celebrate Pentecost. Regardless, it seems very likely that the expression of tongues served two purposes on that day. First, it seems it may have been a divinely empowered personal expression of worship and praise as the recipients were declaring the wonders of God in languages they had not learned. Second, the expression was clearly meant to be a sign and a wonder to others, particularly as it drew in unbelievers to subsequently hear the Gospel.

Having heard these tongues, the effect on the crowd was bewilderment. They were filled with questions and confusion (Acts 2:12). Their tendency was to dismiss the disciples as a bunch of drunken fools (Acts 2:13). Peter, however, seized the opportunity to share the Gospel. It is significant to realize that he seems to do this in his own language, not in tongues. He declares that he and his fellow Christ-followers are not drunk at all. Rather, what everyone was experiencing was the fulfillment of prophecy. *"In the last days, God says, I will pour out my Spirit on all people"* (Acts 2:17, Joel 2:28).

Tongues, in this instance then, served as a sign and a wonder to the unbelievers. It caused them to ask questions and allowed Peter the opportunity to share the Gospel with them. Similarly, Paul writes in 1 Corinthians 14:23 that if unbelievers were to enter Christian gatherings and hear everyone speaking in tongues, they would think that those doing so were all crazy because of their inability to understand what was being said. *"So if the whole church comes together and everyone speaks in tongues, and some who do not understand or some unbelievers come in, will they not say that you are out of your mind?"*

(1 Corinthians 14:23). In this way, the gift of tongues would serve as a wonder that grabs their attention. They would not necessarily be personally benefited by the tongues that were spoken unless those tongues were also coupled with divine interpretation so that everyone could understand what was happening.

TONGUES IN OTHER ACCOUNTS IN ACTS

With the third scriptural mention of tongues, the experience again follows an initial infilling (or baptism) in the Holy Spirit. *"While Peter was still speaking these words, the Holy Spirit came on all who heard the message. The circumcised [Jewish] believers who had come with Peter were astonished that the gift of the Holy Spirit had been poured out even on the Gentiles. For they heard them speaking in tongues and praising God"* (Acts 10:44-46). In this passage, speaking in tongues had to do with offering praises to God. It is important to realize that this group doesn't seem to be speaking to individuals in their own language, rather they are bringing their personal adoration to the Lord. Their unknown tongues are directed solely to Him.

In the next occurrence in Acts, speaking in tongues is again part of the experience of people being filled by the Holy Spirit. Here the speaking is accompanied by another spiritual gift, prophecy. *"When Paul placed his hands on them, the Holy Spirit came on them, and they spoke in tongues and prophesied"* (Acts 19:6).

From each of these historical accounts, it is apparent that often (if not always) the gift of tongues seems to be present when people are initially filled with the Holy Spirit. In the one instance where it is not directly mentioned, speaking in tongues can still be inferred (see Acts 8:14-25). Some people would say that the gift of tongues is therefore "the evidence" of the infilling of the Holy Spirit, but that may be going too far as Scripture does not absolutely declare this to be the case. Moreover, there are outright false religions today that also practice a type of speaking in tongues. It is perhaps more correct to say that speaking in tongues seems scripturally to be one possible and very likely evidence of the infilling of the Holy Spirit. This is why the evidence of being filled with the Spirit should also include an honest display of the fruit of the Spirit and an empowered testimony of Christ, not just spiritual gifts for their own sake.

TONGUES AT CORINTH

The final passage of Scripture that directly addresses the issue of speaking in tongues is found in 1 Corinthians 12-14. This is where the Bible gives us the most direct teaching about what this gift is and how it is meant to operate. In this passage, Paul writes, *"There are different kinds of gifts, but the same Spirit"* (1 Corinthians 12:4). The Greek word that is translated "gifts" is *charismata*, which is built on the root word *charis*. *Charis* is a Greek word that means "grace." Literally, then, speaking in tongues is a "gift of grace."

In one sense, use of this word describes how spiritual gifts come to us. Spiritual gifts are not rewards for godly service, they are not automatic signs of perfected character (which is why we also need the development of the fruit of the Spirit in us), and they are not "proof-positive evidence" of having worked oneself into a place of special "anointing" with God. Far from it! Spiritual gifts are given completely by grace as the Spirit chooses. They are His work. As with any gift, however, we must choose to open and utilize it.

In another sense, this description also depicts what spiritual gifts are meant to impart. Together they are a means of pouring out the grace of God and ministering His peace, comfort, encouragement, strength, healing, direction, joy, deliverance, and more. Spiritual gifts are good and necessary! They come from the Spirit of God. Remember it is Jesus who baptizes us in the Spirit (Matthew 3:11), and to each one of us the manifestation of the Spirit is given (1 Corinthians 12:7), but then it is the Holy Spirit who distributes and enables spiritual gifts in and through us (1 Corinthians 12:11) for the common good. Thus, spiritual gifts are a means of personally both receiving and extending God's divine enablement to others in a tangible way. Surely they can steal our focus if we make them our main emphasis (instead of love, as the Corinthian church discovered), but the Spirit of God has chosen to use them in our lives to impart the touch of the Lord's grace to others. This is why, when directed toward people, speaking in tongues needs to be accompanied with a gift of interpretation. We need spiritual gifts. By inference then, speaking in tongues is quite obviously something good and important in the life of the believer.

In 1 Corinthians 12, we see the gift of tongues being partnered with the gift of interpreting tongues:

> ***Now to each one the manifestation of the Spirit is given for the common good. To one there is given through the Spirit the message of wisdom, to another the message of knowledge by means of the same Spirit, to another faith by the same Spirit, to another gifts of healing by that one Spirit, to another miraculous powers, to another prophecy, to another distinguishing between spirits, to another speaking in different kinds of tongues, and to still another the interpretation of tongues. All these are the work of one and the same Spirit, and he gives them to each one, just as he determines (1 Corinthians 12:7-11).***

The setting has to do with describing the role of spiritual gifts in the life of the Church. At this point, it is appropriate to point out that there seem to be different forms that the gift of tongues can take. The Acts accounts of speaking in tongues and the depictions found in 1 Corinthians have some key differences. Notably, in the book of Acts we never see an example of the partnership that can occur with the gift of speaking in tongues and interpreting tongues. It should probably be better understood that in each of the accounts of Acts where people spoke in tongues, their focus was on speaking to the Lord as a form of prayer and worship and not on speech that was intentionally directed toward other people. Thus, in those cases, an interpretation would not necessarily always be needed as the words were not being offered for the benefit of anyone besides the speaker.

In the Corinthian passage, however, Paul begins to address how these gifts are to be utilized in a corporate sense when the church is gathered. In this context, spiritual gifts are pursued for the common good, and the gift of speaking in tongues is offered in the fashion of public address by the prompting of the Spirit. This type of activity should, therefore, be followed by the gift of interpretation.

The net effect of these gifts being used in this way is to prophesy. In fact, Paul equates the combination of tongues and interpretation with the gift of prophecy. *"He who prophesies is greater than one who speaks in tongues, unless he interprets, so that the church may be edified"* (1 Corinthians 14:5). Prophecy is the spiritual gift through which God speaks directly through one believer (using the person's cooperation, words, and personality) to one or more other people as a way of ministering strength, encouragement, and comfort. Moreover, the two apparently distinct descriptions of the gift of tongues as found in the narrative accounts of Acts and Paul's letter to the Corinthians suggest two different possible utilizations: a personal function (a private prayer language) and a corporate function (a way of supernaturally providing benefit to others when accompanied by the gift of interpretation of tongues). This is again alluded to in 1 Corinthians 14:28, which indicates there is definitely a time and place for speaking in tongues both corporately and in a private, personal sense. *"If anyone speaks in a tongue, two – or at the most three – should speak, one at a time, and someone must interpret. If there is no interpreter, the speaker should keep quiet in the church and speak to himself and God"* (1 Corinthians 14:27-28).

TONGUES AS PART OF OUR PERSONAL EXPRESSION BEFORE THE LORD

Chapter 14 of 1 Corinthians is perhaps the most complete study in the Bible on the purpose and use of the gift of tongues. Verse 2 helps us to understand that speaking in tongues is a process of speaking "mysteries" to God by one's spirit. *"For anyone who speaks in a tongue does not speak to men but to God. Indeed, no one understands him; he utters mysteries with his spirit"* (1 Corinthians 14:2). Paul clarifies this in verse 14, where he indicates that when he prays in tongues, he is praying from his spirit. *"For if I pray in a tongue, my spirit prays, but my mind is unfruitful. So what shall I do? I will pray with my spirit, but I will also pray with my mind; I will sing with my spirit, but I will also sing with my mind"* (1 Corinthians 14:14-15). Notice how this use of speaking in tongues seems to be done as part of Paul's individual and personal practice of prayer and worship.

Because it is speech directed to God Himself, speaking (or even singing!) in tongues becomes an immediate means of communicating with the Lord without benefit to or hindrance by the mind. How helpful this is in times when we are uncertain of how to pray and when human words fail us. It also demonstrates the availability of a personal language of the Spirit that is a source of mystery to the human mind (including the mind of the one speaking) and likely as well as to the enemy. It should be therefore understood that since God is the intended recipient of tongues, the actual sounds being uttered may not necessarily resemble that of any other human language. In other words, it may not necessarily sound like any spoken language that we are accustomed to hearing. No wonder others potentially find it so mysterious! *"For if you have the ability to speak in tongues, you will be talking only to God, since people won't be able to understand you. You will be speaking by the power of the Spirit, but it will all be mysterious"* (1 Corinthians 14:2, NLT).

Verse four tells us that when someone speaks in a tongue, they are built up personally. *"He who speaks in a tongue edifies himself, but he who prophesies edifies the church"* (1 Corinthians 14:4). Why would an individual believer need to be personally edified? At least part of the answer reflects that we are all still caught up in a spiritual battle. We still experience attacks from the evil one. Unbelieving people may be tempted to scoff and ridicule those who follow Christ. We need to learn how to encourage ourselves in the Lord! This admonition reflects the epistle of Jude, where its author reminds us that we are often forced to face those who would rather scoff at the believers and follow their own ungodly desires. How can we face this kind of opposition? Jude writes, *"Build yourselves up in your most holy faith and pray in the Holy Spirit"* (verse 20).

ANSWERING OPPOSITION

Not every Christian agrees with this assessment. Some hold to the idea that the days of spiritual gifts are long past and not even needed in the Church today. They believe that such works of the Spirit have ceased, a doctrine known as "cessationism." These cessation teachers would argue that what Paul is describing in 1 Corinthians 14 is actually a bad thing. Because they hold a bias against speaking in tongues, they perceive the edifying of oneself in this way to be the same as unduly puffing oneself up. That argument, however, is woefully inconsistent with the text. The Greek word used here as "to edify" or "to build up" is always used in a positive way throughout the whole of Scripture. Paul is not describing some prideful act, but rather saying that the gift of tongues builds up and strengthens the *individual* member of the church, whereas prophecy (or tongues with interpretation) builds up the church *corporately*. The suggestion that it is somehow wrong for the individual to be built up is simply an inserted prejudice that is not present in the text and remains inconsistent with the celebration of the gift of tongues that is found in other passages of Scripture. How strange it would be to have a church composed of spiritually emaciated members because it was in some way wrong for them to be individually edified!

Cessationists also tend to describe the gift of tongues in the Bible as a supernatural ability to present the Gospel to those who speak a different language. They argue that this is no longer needed since we can now print Bibles in most of the current languages of the world. How unfortunate for that argument, however, is the fact that speaking in tongues was absolutely never utilized in this way anywhere in Scripture. There are no biblical accounts where this happens! You will not find a story where Paul preached in tongues on any of his missionary churches in order to better connect with the indigenous population. It simply did not occur. Tongues is primarily a means of communication between the individual and God, and then sometimes used to bless and edify the larger Church body when coupled with the gift of interpretation.

At the same time, we should note that enabling anyone to suddenly speak in a foreign human language is an act that God could certainly perform. It is surely within His ability, and there may perhaps be examples of such instances recorded in history (both ancient and recent), but this would be better classified in the 1 Corinthians 12 list of spiritual gifts as a "miracle," and not necessarily as part of any general understanding of the gift of tongues. Consider also that when it was time to present the Gospel in Acts 2 to a crowd of people from numerous surrounding nations, Peter didn't do so by preaching in tongues but by speaking in a language everyone could understand.

The gift of tongues is not typically utilized in Scripture as the supernatural ability to communicate in someone else's language. Though that seems to have happened on the day of Pentecost, that is not how the gift was used in any other biblical account. If speaking in tongues were primarily understood to operate in this way, there would be no need for the gift of interpretation! Additionally, what would then be the point of speaking someone else's language "to oneself" as instructed in 1 Corinthians 14:28? Rather, speaking in tongues is a means of speaking mysteries to God by the Spirit for the primary purpose of building up the individual believer.

EMBRACING AN EAGER MINDSET

Of overall significance in 1 Corinthians 14 is Paul's urging that we intentionally pursue those gifts that build up the church. *"Since you are eager to have spiritual gifts, try to excel in gifts that build up the church"* (1 Corinthians 14:12). As we do this, the apostle is not decrying the use or pursuit of tongues. Rather, he seems to be saying, "Don't stop with just that one gift. Instead, be zealously passionate about pursuing all kinds of spiritual gifts. Go after them all! Just make sure that the goal at all times is love!" *"Follow the way of love and eagerly desire spiritual gifts"* (1 Corinthians 14:1). In other words, more than speaking in tongues, also be eager to prophesy. Ask to interpret tongues so the church can be built up!

Paul also notes that even when he speaks in tongues, his own mind does not understand it (1 Corinthians 14:14). We are meant to note as we read this that he personally practices praying and singing in tongues as part of his own personal expression to the Lord. When his words are directed to the church, however, he prays, sings, and teaches from his mind and with his understanding so that others can fathom what is being said (1 Corinthians 14:15-18). Some take this as indicating that no one should ever speak in tongues in the church, as if the phrase "in the church" means "once the service has started" or "among the believers." This is hardly the case! Is it wrong, then, to offer up a private prayer in the midst of a corporate gathering? Certainly not. More accurately, is it ever appropriate to offer up an individual expression of praise despite the presence of other believers in Christ? Of course it is! But these individual expressions should never override the prayer and praise that is being offered publicly. And certainly, then, when addressing the church, tongues (without interpretation) would not be fitting since it is something that should be first and foremost directed to the Lord. This is confirmed in verses 26-28 where various means of other corporate instruction and participation are listed such as the sharing of hymns, instructions, revelations, and tongues with interpretation. *"What then shall we say, brothers? When you come together, everyone has a hymn, or a word of instruction, a revelation, a tongue or an interpretation. All of these must be done for the strengthening of the church"* (1 Corinthians 14:26).

HOW CAN I SPEAK IN TONGUES?

So how does one come to speak in tongues? This is a different question than "How does one learn to speak in tongues?" In fact, I would argue that it is something which cannot be learned. At times, some Christians, even ministers, from their own determination and zeal to make something happen, have unfortunately encouraged others to begin speaking in tongues by utilizing random syllables as a way of "priming the pump." This is ill-advised. Speaking in tongues is an activity initially originated by the Spirit and is only one of the many possible effects and outcomes of being filled with the Holy Spirit. May we instead trust the Lord to have His way in His time as He directs.

Jesus tells us in the gospel of Luke that the Father simply gives the Holy Spirit to them that ask. *"Which of you fathers, if your son asks for a fish, will give him a snake instead? Or if he asks for an egg, will give him a scorpion? If you then, though you are evil, know how to give good gifts to your children, how much more will your Father in heaven give the Holy Spirit to those who ask him!"* (Luke 11:11-13).

All those who have surrendered their lives to Christ and turned from their sins can ask the Father to saturate (baptize) them with the Holy Spirit. It is an outpouring from the Lord Jesus that we receive by faith and one that we can and should regularly participate in over and over again. *"Do not get drunk on wine, which leads to debauchery. Instead, be filled with the Spirit"* (Ephesians 5:18). The Amplified Bible brings out some of the original Greek nuances of this verse by saying, *"but ever be filled and stimulated with the [Holy] Spirit."* One byproduct of such filling is the release of spiritual gifts, including speaking in tongues.

The experience of speaking in tongues varies with each individual receiving it, and there is no set rule given in Scripture. Some people have had other believers lay their hands on them to receive. Others receive while listening to a sermon or while worshiping (either corporately or by themselves). Some people feel overcome with emotion and experience a tangible "feeling" of the Spirit. Others experience very little emotion or perhaps no tangible feelings at all, yet they will begin to speak in tongues. Some seem to sense only one or two words at first with more following later as they faithfully utter these words, while still others seem to receive fluent, multiple syllables and phrases. Some people report hearing sounds in their heads which they then choose to speak. Others report it as more of a sensation that seems to arise from their mid-section or "belly."

Almost universally, speaking in tongues is not reported as being something that is uncontrollable or a force that takes over a person's tongue. People simply ask the Lord Jesus to baptize them in the Holy Spirit, expect to speak in tongues, and then walk in obedience as they understand themselves to be receiving this gift. There is often a "leap-of-faith" moment where the recipient must choose to trust that what they are experiencing is from the Holy Spirit and then decide to begin speaking as the Spirit enables them.

Once a believer has received the gift of speaking in tongues, he or she should be able to pray in tongues at will as a personal "prayer language" for the purpose of building themselves up in the Lord. In fact, such practice is to be encouraged as part of both a daily devotional time before God as well as during ongoing, "in-the-moment" prayers throughout the day or in times of intercession and spiritual warfare.

Of course, the obvious question is "What about those who ask and then who do not speak in tongues?" Does this mean that the gift of tongues is not for them? Let's not even remotely think so! The Scripture has much to say about prayer and perseverance. Any believer who has asked to be baptized in the Holy Spirit but has not also yet experienced speaking in tongues should be patient and continue to make it a matter of prayer, but at the same time not become worried or obsessed. We receive the baptism in the Holy Spirit by faith, and the Lord has promised to give the Spirit to those who ask. In this way, we can trust that the Lord has baptized us. The gift of tongues may simply not have emerged yet, but it very well could at a future time. In the meantime, focus on excelling in the fruit of the Spirit: love, joy, peace, patience, gentleness, goodness, meekness, self-control and faithfulness (Galatians 5:22-23). Simply continue to seek the Lord and allow Him to work in you as He determines!

Keep in mind, being able to speak in tongues does not necessarily mean that someone is a better, holier Christian. It does not mean that God likes them more. It does not mean that they are more spiritual than someone else. It does mean, however, that they are simply manifesting the grace to be built up and internally strengthened in greater measure. It's now up to each person to walk in that grace, and that will invariably involve much more than simply speaking in tongues.

Speaking in tongues is but one device in the spiritual toolbox that the Spirit wants to use to better fulfill the Lord's purposes for our lives. When used rightly, it becomes a powerful means for growing and finding strength in the Lord. When elevated above other gifts and above the need to simultaneously submit our character to the Holy Spirit's work, it can become a divisive display of pride that causes contention among those jockeying for some kind of spiritual position. The truth is that even speaking in known tongues, an understood language, remains hard enough. We need the Spirit's help for just that! James declares, *"If anyone is never at fault in what he says, he is a perfect man, able to keep his whole body in check,"* and *"the tongue is a small part of the body, but it makes great boasts. Consider what a great forest is set on fire by a small spark"* (James 3:2,5). Oh, how we all need Spirit empowerment on our lips! Paul adds, *"If I speak in the tongues of men and of angels, but have not love, I am only a resounding gong or a clanging cymbal"* (1 Corinthians 13:1). The solution to such issues is not to become either boastful or passive about speaking tongues, but rather to love the Lord our God and then love others even as we love ourselves so that this gift does not become a divisive issue between believers.

CONCLUSION

The bottom line is that Paul says not to forbid speaking in tongues (1 Corinthians 14:39). Beyond that, he also tells us to zealously pursue spiritual gifts (1 Corinthians 14:1). In verses 29 and 30 of 1 Corinthians 12, Paul asks, *"Are all apostles? Are all prophets? Are all teachers? Do all work miracles? Do all have gifts of healing? Do all speak in tongues? Do all interpret?"* The implied answer is "no." Even so, in the context of these verses, Paul's reference to tongues seems to be that sense in which an address is being made corporately in tongues and meant to be followed by an interpretation. It is not necessarily apparent that he is referring to the personal experience of tongues. While it is true that not every believer will speak in tongues, that does not, therefore, mean that the Scripture is also declaring that Christian people should not or cannot all speak in tongues in their personal prayers and expression before the Lord (as if some of us do not need to be built up in our inner being). Let's not conclude that we do not need this gift. Rather, may those who speak in tongues continue to do so with all their heart and find strength in the Lord, and may those who do not yet speak in tongues continue to posture themselves openly before the Holy Spirit trusting that He indeed distributes spiritual gifts as He decides. May we remain eager for this gift to be unleashed in each of us and for each of us to be built up in the faith.

"But eagerly desire the greater gifts. And now I will show you the most excellent way" (1 Corinthians 12:31).

PAUSE AND REFLECT:

What is your gut reaction to the idea of speaking in tongues?

- ❏ Passionately engaged
- ❏ Practicing occasionally
- ❏ Eager and hopeful
- ❏ Curious and intrigued
- ❏ Indifferent
- ❏ Disillusioned
- ❏ Disbelieving
- ❏ Fearful

With the above response, what do you see as your next step in experiencing and expressing this gift?

How has this chapter's journey through the Scriptures impacted your understanding of speaking in tongues?

What words of encouragement might you offer to someone who is feeling like a second-rate Christian because they haven't spoken in tongues?

How might you better incorporate speaking in tongues as part of your personal prayer and worship before the Lord?

Part 2
The Ministry of the Spirit in the Local Church

The previous chapters have clearly demonstrated that the Lord is looking to raise up Spirit-empowered disciples through whom others are strengthened and brought into the kingdom of God. Jesus ministered in the power of the Spirit with tremendous results. He is the model for how we are to live by the Spirit. He baptizes us in the Holy Spirit so that we might have power to be effective witnesses for Him everywhere we go. With the fruit of the Spirit, the Lord transforms our character and conforms us more and more into His image. With spiritual gifts, He enables us to touch the world with signs and wonders and to promote the common good. However, we must remember that the Lord is not only looking to empower individuals, He is also building His Church. Together, we are the body of Christ.

Throughout the book of Acts, we see not only the ministry of the Holy Spirit through the apostles, but also the establishing and strengthening of local churches in an ever-broadening circle as the message of the Gospel grows and deepens in them. When we understand that a significant part of God's plan to reach the world is through the example and ministry of the local church, a series of questions arise. How does the local church emphasize and prioritize the move of the Holy Spirit in a healthy way? Are there unhealthy ways to pursue the move of the Spirit? Are there guidelines and parameters that local church leaders should consider as they call people to embrace Jesus as Lord and to be eager for the move of the Spirit in and through their lives? What directives can we find in the Scripture?

When it comes to understanding the baptism in the Holy Spirit and the display of spiritual gifts in the local church, the Scriptures provide us with at least two kinds of literature from which we can discover important guidelines: "teaching" and "history." It is important that we thoroughly explore both types of literature in order to get a well-rounded perspective.

The letters of Paul are our primary source for finding detailed directions and input about how the ministry of the Spirit can and should look in a local church. The information and commands found in 1 Corinthians 12-14 serve as the very essence of such teaching and they have much to say to us today. In fact, Paul writes at length concerning the gifts and workings of the Spirit using a couple of Greek terms to sum them up.

The first is kind of a summary term: *pneumatikos* (literally "spirituals," "spiritual gifts," or "that which generally has to do with the Spirit" as found in 1 Corinthians 12:1, 14:1). The second is *charismata* (literally, "gifts of grace" or "that which is freely and graciously given and bestowed" as found in Romans 12:6; 1 Corinthians 12:9; and 12:31. Both words have to do with the powerful workings of the Holy Spirit that are graciously given to help those in need or to display the Lord's favor and kindness. *Charismata* tends to be a bit more specific. It is used in 1 Corinthians 12:9 where Paul mentions that the Spirit gives *"to another gifts of healing,"* indicating a supernatural working of grace that manifests as healing. At the same time, 1 Corinthians 14:1 declares, *"Follow the way of love and eagerly desire spiritual gifts (pneumatikos)."* The verse serves as a reminder that any pursuit of the supernatural workings of the Spirit must remain centered in genuine love. Otherwise, we can become unduly preoccupied by the pursuit of supernatural display. Do we pursue spiritual gifts simply for the gifts' sake or out of some prideful desire to present ourselves as some sort of spiritual elitist? Neither reason is good enough. Our spiritual pursuits must rather serve the cause of love first and foremost! If we are not careful, however, we can begin to chase after spiritual gifts because we long for the experiences of power or to see *charismata* and *pneumatikos* on display for the sheer excitement of it.

Local ministry in Charismatic and Pentecostal churches has often included experiences that are difficult to explain. Some people feel overcome by the presence of the Spirit and fall to the ground. Others may literally run around the church. Some might cry out in what sounds like moaning and great travail, while others can become unusually quiet, even fixed in a trance. There are countless experiences that are attributed to the workings of the Holy Spirit that can be surprising to our eyes and not clearly represented in the Bible. How can a local church navigate its way as it looks to embrace all that God wants to do while perhaps finding itself at times in the midst of ministry happenings that are otherwise hard to articulate, let alone explain to others? We will take a look at such phenomena more closely, but as we work to pursue a way forward that intends to honor the Lord and not quench the move of the Spirit, we should also consider another type of literature that we find in the Bible in addition to the writings of Paul: the history of the Church.

As we review the stories of the early believers and the developing New Testament Church and carefully study how they embraced and pursued the ministry of the

Spirit themselves, we can begin to piece together guidelines that can help shape us today. That might not be as straightforward as it first seems. The truth is that the move of the Spirit took on somewhat different emphases as the Church expanded into new locales. Reflecting on the examples found in each place can help us to better discern best practices for today's Church.

The early believers were the first to be impacted by the outpouring of the Holy Spirit. How did they respond? How did they grow? In what ways did the ministry of the Spirit develop in them and in the life of the Church? As we contemplate the answers, let's go back to those early days. In the New Testament we have an opportunity to take a close look at the ministry of the Spirit as the new believers developed maturity over time in their response to Him. In accounts from the initial move in Jerusalem to the outpouring in Antioch of Syria to Ephesus to Corinth and beyond, there are lessons that we can incorporate into our contemporary settings. Let's explore those lessons in some detail and consider how best to apply them today.

Chapter 5
Embracing the Move of the Spirit:
Lessons from the Church in Jerusalem

On the day of Pentecost, the believers were gathered in Jerusalem. It was there that the baptism in the Holy Spirit originally occurred. It was in Jerusalem that the church began to quickly grow, not only in numbers and maturity but also in its experience of the workings of the Spirit. We surely have something to learn from their example. This is where the Church first began to come together and function as a body of believers. Clear examples of charismata in Acts can be seen in Jerusalem (Acts 2-7) where the church was formed as a direct result of the Spirit's outpouring on the day of Pentecost. Let's take a moment to revisit these examples and then consider what lessons we might find as we look to fan into flame the ministry of the Spirit in our own churches today.

REVISITING ACTS 2

The outpouring of the Holy Spirit upon those gathered in the upper room in Jerusalem (Acts 2:1-13) was a powerful event prophesied by Jesus that enabled God's people to carry out the mission presented in Acts 1:8 – to be Christ's witnesses in Jerusalem, Judea, Samaria, and to the ends of the earth. The event was marked by a series of Spirit phenomena. There was the sound of a violent wind (Acts 2:2). What visibly appeared to be tongues of fire came to rest on those present (Acts 2:3). All who were in the room were suddenly filled with the Holy Spirit (Acts 2:4). They all began to speak "in other tongues" as the Spirit enabled them (Acts 2:4).

These "tongues" can be understood in at least two ways. On the one hand, the gift of being able to speak actual languages previously unknown to the speaker seems to certainly be on display (especially since each person in the surrounding crowd heard his or her own language) while on the other hand there may have also been the simultaneous utterance of speech that was completely unintelligible to others who were passing by. This is evidenced by the charge from some in the crowd that those speaking must have been "drunk" (verse 13). Though the sound of the rushing wind and the observation of visible fire does not occur again in the Scriptures, speaking in tongues continued to be manifest in subsequent accounts of Holy Spirit outpourings (Acts 10:46; Acts 19:6).

Following this initial Pentecost event, other examples of spiritual gifts in action began to occur. Peter preached to the crowd and quoted from Joel 2, declaring that *charismata* such as prophecy, visions, and divine dreams would all result from this outpouring of the Spirit (Acts 2:17). As part of this message, Peter was certainly proclaiming that those who embrace life in Christ (and therefore life in the Spirit) can expect to be sustained and empowered by this overall gift of the Spirit until Jesus returns. He certainly indicates that this expectation and experience is available to people in all stages of life: both sons and daughters, both the old and the young, both male and female servants (and therefore every class of people). All of us are meant to live by the power and presence of the Spirit. This truth is made very plain as Peter continued to preach the message about Jesus and as the crowd became stirred and cried out, wanting to know how they should best respond (Acts 2:37). Peter instructed them to repent and be baptized in the name of Jesus with the promise that they would receive *"the gift of the Holy Spirit,"* just as it had been prophesied by the prophet Joel. In response, three thousand people suddenly made the choice to repent and

> **PAUSE AND REFLECT:**
>
> In your church practice, what could be the benefits of simultaneously emphasizing these three facets from Peter's sermon: salvation, repentance, and the gift of the Holy Spirit?
>
> How could you actively emphasize the gift of the Spirit for both men and women? Both the old and the young (even children)?
>
> How might your church connect current outpouring experiences to power for daily living and personal growth?

became followers of Jesus. The church in Jerusalem was born (Acts 2:41)! When reading this account, we are meant to understand that believers in Jesus should expect to now live by the sustaining presence of the Spirit with corresponding supernatural manifestations of His presence. By the infilling of the Spirit, there is the empowerment for living a new life and for effectively sharing the Gospel message.

SPIRIT-EMPOWERED MINISTRY IN JERUSALEM

In Acts 2:42-47, during the days after Pentecost, we find a depiction of how this new daily life in the Spirit can look. The believers devoted themselves to the apostles' teaching and to fellowship, to the breaking of bread, and to prayer (Acts 2:42). They stayed close to one another and shared their belongings in common, even selling possessions in order to better care for each one in need (Acts 2:44-45). They purposefully met together every day in the Temple courts and then shared meals in each other's homes (Acts 2:46-47). This narrative of everyday life is meant to show us how a true relational community had been made possible as a direct result of the outpouring of the Spirit. It could be said that the impact of the Spirit's infilling is such that those so affected were now marked by a new way of living: *love*. Fascinatingly, ongoing supernatural signs and wonders then continued to occur through the apostles (Acts 2:43). The whole passage provides a description of a "new normal" – a new kind of daily life. By reading the story, we are witness to the miraculous formation of the Church with *charismata* clearly in action!

This was just the beginning. Specific instances of charismata in the new Jerusalem church continued to take place. A lame man was healed as Peter and John went to the temple to pray (Acts 3:1-10). Peter preached with renewed inspiration to the ruling Jewish elders by the power of the Spirit (Acts 4:8-13). After prayer, the place where the people of God were gathered was literally shaken as they were all again filled with the Spirit and spoke the Word of God boldly (Acts 4:31). These outward experiences of transformation were joined by deepening inward ones as the believers came together with one heart and mind to share everything they had in order to make sure that no one among them was left in need (Acts 4:32-35). So important was this value of Spirit-empowered relational care that when Ananias and Sapphira each decided to act selfishly and then tried to lie to the church (and thereby to the Holy Spirit), they both were confronted by Peter and subsequently fell down dead (Acts 5:1-10)! Honest, transparent, others-centered care was a central component of the move of the Spirit.

At the same time, great signs and wonders continued as the apostles ministered among the people (Acts 5:12). Numerous sick and demonized people were brought from surrounding towns, and all were healed (Acts 5:15-16)! When the apostles were suddenly arrested by the high priest, an angel of the Lord miraculously released them during the night and enabled them to return to their ministry in the streets (Acts 5:17-21). All these events showcase a great display of power by the Spirit through and on behalf of the apostles as they led the church. It seems, however, that Acts 6 brought a new development.

When logistical problems began to arise in the church regarding the daily distribution of food to the widows, the solution was for the people to find additional men who were *"full of the Spirit and wisdom"* who could take on the responsibility (Acts 6:3) of ensuring quality care. Such men included Stephen, a man *"full of faith and of the Holy Spirit"* (Acts 6:5). These individuals were brought before the apostles, who prayed and laid their hands on them as they were commissioned into their roles (Acts 6:6). The impact throughout the church was immediate. Spirit-empowered disciples were released to demonstrate the love of God by providing ongoing care to those who were in desperate need. At the same time, the Word of God spread all the more as the apostles were released to give their attention to prayer and proclamation (Acts 6:4,7). All of this resulted in a sharp increase in the number of Jerusalem disciples. Then, as the narrative shifts to focus more closely on Stephen, we find another significant note regarding the exercise of *charismata* and *pneumatikos*.

Luke adds an additional, specific description of Stephen, calling him a man *"full of God's grace and power"* (Acts 6:8). Such grace enabled Stephen to perform *"great wonders and signs among the people"* (Acts 6:8). While the specifics of such signs are not given to us, it is interesting to note that such terminology in Acts so far has been used only to describe the supernatural ministry of Jesus (Acts 2:22), followed by that of the apostles after the day of Pentecost (as previously discussed). Now we become witness to the supernatural activity flowing through others in the Church! Furthermore, when facing confrontational members from the local Jewish synagogue, the Scripture tells us that Stephen experienced supernatural wisdom by the Spirit that enabled him to answer every objection (Acts 6:10). Clearly, the Scripture is giving witness to the manifestation of charismata, gifts of grace, through someone who was not one of the original followers of Jesus but who had become converted and discipled in the church of Jerusalem. This is a distinct change, demonstrating the flow of charismata through more than just the apostles.

After being seized by a mob and charged falsely before the Sanhedrin, somehow (by the power of the Spirit?) Stephen's countenance appeared to them as *"the face of an angel"* (Acts 6:15). As the leaders gnashed their teeth at him, Luke tells us that Stephen was (again) full of the Holy Spirit and enabled to look up to heaven where he could supernaturally see *"the glory of God, and Jesus standing at the right hand of God,"* a sight which he then boldly declared before his accusers (Acts 7:55-56).

With this account, we also become witness of a fulfillment (perhaps in microcosm) of what Peter had earlier declared before the crowd on the day of Pentecost. The Holy Spirit had been poured out on a young man, Stephen, who saw a vision and then prophesied! *Charismata* in action! As the incensed Sanhedrin members then rushed to stone him, perhaps an even greater evidence of Spirit infilling was revealed as Stephen's dying words asked the Lord to *"not hold this sin against them"* (Acts 7:60). What forgiveness! What grace! What power!

IMPLICATIONS FOR CONTEMPORARY MINISTRY

In 1 Corinthians 12:31, right in the middle of an extended discourse on spiritual gifts, the Apostle Paul writes, *"But eagerly desire the greater gifts. And now I will show you the most excellent way."* With that, he enters into a powerful discussion on love. This love is not to be understood as an alternative to spiritual gifts, but rather is to be the *"way"* (or the *atmosphere, culture,* and *temperament*) that must continually surround the ministry of spiritual gifts. In this way, the "best" gifts are those which are centered in the love of God. Such gifts are others-centered and work to build others up. While God remains sovereign over the distribution of all spiritual gifts, it is apparent that believers should be zealous and even pray specifically to deploy certain gifts rather than passively wait for them to appear.

All through the discussion of the Spirit working through the church in Jerusalem, the overriding motivation of love remains apparent. Displays of *charismata* and the overall *pneumatikos* of the Spirit continually served the greater good of helping the members of the Church as well as touching the surrounding outsiders in order to help them turn to Christ. Such giftings and miraculous encounters are never presented as markings of individual greatness or piety on some imaginary spirituality scoreboard, but rather center on how to best serve others in an effort to draw them to Christ and to bless them with kindness and mercy as a reflection of the love of God. If it does anything at all, the work of the Holy Spirit through the life of any believer (and any church) is meant to put the unconditional love of God on display!

A striking aspect of this love and its connection to the flow of *charismata* in the life of the church in Jerusalem was the intentional and frequent regularity of the believers pursuing quality relationship with one another. The Acts 2 narrative is overwhelmingly clear. Verses 42-47 give us several powerful and insightful summations. The people *devoted* themselves to the apostles' teaching, to *fellowship* with one another, to the *breaking of bread*, and to *prayer*. *Every day* they continued to meet *together* in the temple courts. *"They broke bread in their homes and ate together with glad and sincere hearts, praising God . . . and the Lord added to their number daily."* By the time the reader gets to Acts 4:32, the believers had become *one* in heart and mind and were deliberately looking to meet the needs of anyone who was impoverished among them. By Acts 6, this heart had blossomed into a *daily* commitment to make sure all the widows had enough food to eat.

The point is that the display of *charismata* by the apostles and by Stephen (and perhaps others) was found within an intentional church-wide atmosphere of love. In Jerusalem, it was apparent they had captured the most excellent way. In contemporary ministry, especially among Pentecostals and Charismatics, we may already have a determined chasing of *charismata* and *pneumatikos*, but without the intentional, self-sacrificing prioritizing of love and community, this pursuit may very well serve to be of no lasting consequence. At all times, love must remain our motivation and be our overarching guideline to Spirit-filled ministry. Otherwise, it misses the mark and simply becomes a chasing after supernatural display for the sake of power and image.

The outpouring of the Spirit in the church of Jerusalem reveals the importance of a central lesson: the move of the Spirit must be centered in the incredible love of the Father. This lesson was foundational for all that was yet to come. By exploring the spread of the Gospel and the move of the Spirit to places beyond Jerusalem, additional lessons can certainly be observed. However, without love being the continual priority, everything else becomes inconsequential. If there is going to be a true thriving in the Spirit in the practices and administration of our churches, we must hold fast to the biblical admonition to love others as much as we love ourselves.

> **PAUSE AND REFLECT:**
>
> How does your church anticipate and expect the gift of speaking in tongues as associated with the infilling of the Holy Spirit? How is this gift encouraged and given opportunity among your congregation? What might constitute a loving way to promote this gift without creating undue pressure?
>
> Why might the showcase of "love" be such a central component to the ministry of the Spirit?
>
> Is **loving** a word that accurately describes your church and the atmosphere of your gatherings? Why do you think that is? What could help this even more?
>
> In what ways can your church's emphasis on the move of the Holy Spirit also contribute to intentional ways for the members to relationally connect, encourage, and serve one another?
>
> If an outsider were to observe your church's teaching and practice regarding the ministry of the Spirit, would they be more inclined to think that it was about having powerful experiences during meetings, or about becoming empowered to love and serve others between meetings? Is there anything you would like to change about that perception? What next steps might you and your leadership prayerfully consider?

Chapter 6
Following the Move of the Spirit:
From Jerusalem to Antioch

The account of the move of the Spirit throughout the book of Acts is powerful to read and study. The events that took place on the Day of Pentecost had significant impact on both the 120 disciples gathered in the upper room and the crowd that observed it all when those disciples spilled out into the street. These first recipients of the baptism in the Holy Spirit were full of praise and full of courage. The Spirit's outpouring enabled Peter to preach to the crowd with great conviction and anointing. The crowd could not help but be drawn into what was being presented. The workings of the Spirit were demonstrable; they garnered attention. None of it, however, was simply about a supernatural display for its own sake. Rather, the move of the Spirit that day ultimately served to advance the message of salvation as it was presented by Peter and as three thousand people repented of their sins and gave their lives to Christ.

There was a supernatural partnership that day between the Spirit and the disciples. As the opportunity arose, Peter stepped up to proclaim the message of Jesus and to call the crowd to listen carefully to what he was saying. The move of the Spirit through the lives of individual people, whether it be the believers back then or us today, is meant to energize believers and give credibility for the Gospel message of salvation. As Spirit-empowered believers recognize the importance of the opportunities that God provides, the presence and power of the Spirit grows beyond a source of personal transformation and begins to impact the larger community. Isn't this our hope for the ministry of the Holy Spirit in our churches today? Do we have God-ordained vision for the Gospel to advance in this fashion? To get there, are we willing to look beyond "Jerusalem" and bring the kingdom of God every place we go? A thriving relationship with the Holy Spirit includes embracing the Spirit's heart for the world and learning to recognize and act on the moments God provides to proclaim Christ to the world around us.

MOVING BEYOND JERUSALEM

The outpouring of the Holy Spirit in Jerusalem was a launching point for the Church. While the church there grew in numbers and influence, the Lord was also planning to advance the Gospel to people who were in far-off lands. In Acts chapter 8, we are told that a great persecution broke out against the church in Jerusalem resulting in believers escaping to numerous other places across Judea, Samaria, and beyond. Along the way, wherever they went, these early believers continued to preach the Word, and the Holy Spirit continued to move powerfully among them. For example, the ministry of the Spirit through Philip included delivering people of evil spirits and bringing healing to those who were paralyzed or suffered other disabilities. These events caused the people to listen even more closely to the message he proclaimed and to put their trust in Christ. One of these early converts was Simon, a man who had practiced sorcery.

> **PAUSE AND REFLECT:**
>
> Have an honest conversation with your leaders. Does your church desire to flow in the presence and power of the Spirit? Why? What is the motivation? Are you hoping to simply advance the name of your church and ministry? Are you trying to compete with another area ministry? How do you measure success?
>
> How do you envision the active ministry of the Holy Spirit helping to advance the Gospel in your area? Are you and your fellow leaders in agreement about what you believe is God's vision for the people in your community?
>
> Just as Peter and John added to the ministry of Philip by laying hands on people to receive the Holy Spirit, what priority does this kind of ministry take in your setting? In what ways can your church help bring opportunities for people to be baptized in the Spirit as they choose to trust in Jesus?

Exposed to the undeniable move of the Spirit through Philip, Simon opened his heart to the Gospel and was even baptized. Later, when Peter and John arrived in the same area, they noted that the Spirit had *"not yet come upon any"* of the new believers (Acts 8:16). When they prayed and laid hands on the people, they received the Holy Spirit! Simon was immediately captivated by what he saw, but his desires and ambitions were not yet fully submitted to the Lord. He was drawn to power for power's sake. He previously had been renowned for his exploits in dark magic and had been revered by all the people because of it. Now he saw an opportunity to continue to promote himself through the ministry of the Spirit. He even offered money to the apostles to give him this power, but Peter rebuked him sternly. Simon the sorcerer had become a believer and was drawn to the move of the Holy Spirit, but the need for continued transformation remained. His intent to utilize the ministry of the Spirit for personal promotion and gain made it clear to the apostles that he was still captive to sin and in need of deeper repentance. Meanwhile, Peter and John *"testified and proclaimed the word of the Lord"* as they continued traveling from community to community. Their focus was not on making a name for themselves. Rather, their efforts stayed centered on how to best proclaim the Gospel as empowered by the Spirit.

THE CHURCH IN ANTIOCH

Acts 11 tells us that some of the believers who had scattered away from Jerusalem because of persecution also landed in Antioch. Antioch, which was around 300 miles north of Jerusalem, was one of the largest cities in Syria and was considered "the capital of the east"; at least, that was the phrase printed on its own coins. Although a segment of the population of Antioch was Jewish, it was primarily a Gentile city and therefore predominately pagan. The overall belief system of the people did not generally include recognizing, let alone worshiping, the God of Abraham, Isaac, and Jacob. This fact, however, only makes the work of the Holy Spirit among those people all the more miraculous and astounding.

To this point in the book of Acts, the ministry of the Church had not yet been fully extended to the Gentiles. There had been isolated cases of Gentile conversions such as with the Ethiopian eunuch and the household of Cornelius (who received the outpouring of the Spirit while Peter was in the middle of preaching to them), but the disciples had not yet fully expected the message of the Gospel to reach the Gentiles in large numbers. In Antioch, however, all that began to change. Jesus had told His followers that when the Holy Spirit came upon them, they would receive power and be His witnesses in Jerusalem, Judea, Samaria, and to the ends of the earth (Acts 1:8). With Antioch, the "ends of the earth" portion of the prophecy began to be fulfilled.

While some of the believers who were escaping persecution brought the message to the Jews in Antioch, additional believers from Cyprus and Cyrene carried the good news about the Lord Jesus to the Gentiles. The result was that great numbers from both people groups believed and turned to the Lord. In this way, the church of Antioch was created and began to meet regularly, a feat that was nothing short of astonishing! For the first time in history, significantly large groups of both Jews and Gentiles (who ordinarily could not stand one another) had come into Christ and were worshiping together repeatedly! The Holy Spirit was moving powerfully among the people, but the sudden growth resulted in a church full of "baby" believers without a preexisting foundation of teaching and understanding about either Jesus or the Spirit. For many (and likely most) of them, their previous spiritual understanding was full of false truths and pagan beliefs. As they came into the kingdom of God, they needed training and instruction. They needed pastoring. They needed a system of Spirit-led direction to keep them on the right track and to help them continue in Spirit-empowered living. They needed leadership.

THE NEED FOR LEADERSHIP

The news of what the Spirit was doing in Antioch was so significant that it soon traveled all the way back to the church in Jerusalem. The leaders there responded by sending Barnabas to both investigate and help. He could not have been a more perfect choice. He was a Levite from Cyprus. His Levitical heritage would help him connect with the Jewish believers. Originating from Cyprus, however, Barnabas would also have a great basis for connecting with the Greek and Gentile believers who had come into the Kingdom through the believers who had come from Cyprus as well.

Barnabas is first mentioned in the Scripture near the end of Acts 4. He was known then by a different name, Joseph. Understanding the role of "Joseph" as a Levite has tremendous significance when we consider the events of Acts 4. The Levites assisted the priests and leaders with public worship. They were musicians, guardians, temple officials, gatekeepers, craftsmen, and more. They did whatever was required of them to help the priests lead, offer sacrifices, and conduct their duties. The Scripture tells us that of all the tribes of Israel who came to occupy the land of Canaan, the Levites were not allowed to own property. The land was not to be considered their inheritance, for the Lord Himself would be their inheritance (Joshua 13:33).

Let's remember the context of this period of time. Immediately after Peter and John were released from jail (having been imprisoned overnight for healing a lame man and for preaching to the crowd about Jesus), the church had come together to pray for even more signs and wonders and for boldness to declare the Gospel. As they were all filled anew by the Spirit, the believers became unified, sharing one heart and mind. Led by the Spirit, they began to look for ways to care for one another so that no one among them would be found in need. Joseph sold a field that he owned and laid it at the apostles' feet. This action shows us the significant change that had taken place in his heart. Not only had he become a believer in Jesus, but he also was looking to come into a place of true obedience before the Lord. Levites were not supposed to own property, and so Joseph likely sold his field as an act of contrition and repentance. Additionally, he chose not to profit from the sale, but to instead bless and encourage the church. The Scripture notes that he underwent a name change from Joseph, meaning "God will give," to Barnabas, which means "son of encouragement." If anyone could be considered an encourager to the church, especially at great sacrifice, it was certainly true of Barnabas.

It seems the leaders of the church in Jerusalem understood that the Antioch believers might need encouragement. They might need special assistance. They might need wise leadership to help them steward all that was happening . . . and Barnabas was the one for the job.

When Barnabas arrived in Antioch, the Scripture tells us that he saw for himself *"the evidence of the grace* [Greek = charis] *of God"* (Acts 11:23). What was this "evidence of the grace"? Perhaps it was simply the number of people who were responding to the Gospel. Perhaps it was the display and ministry of "grace-gifts" among the people (charis-mata). Certainly, it included the wonderous way Jews and Gentiles continued to come together in joint worship before the Lord! How Barnabas responded provides some lessons for us all. First, he was glad. He celebrated all that God was doing in this new ministry that defied their previous expectations. Second, he encouraged them. Of course he did! That's exactly the kind of person he was! Moreover, Acts 11:24 tells us that he was *"a good man, full of the Holy Spirit and faith."* So, what happened after Barnabas began to encourage the church to remain true to the Lord? Even greater numbers of people became followers of Jesus! Transformation was happening in individual hearts and in the region as a whole. What an amazing and influential time!

FANNING THE WIND OF THE SPIRIT INTO GREATER FLAME

Have you ever tried to start a fire without the use of artificial accelerants? You don't begin with large chunks of wood, but rather with kindling. Little scraps and shavings, small sticks and twigs, bits of paper, cloth, and the like are carefully assembled and struck with a heat source, whether that be the friction of rubbing sticks together or the spark of a flint. As those little bits of tinder begin to ignite, the addition of moving air helps the embers to catch flame. The more kindling that ignites the more it can be fanned into an even greater flame, allowing for larger wood pieces to be added until a fire is blazing. Using this metaphor in his second letter to Timothy, the Apostle Paul instructed the young pastor to fan into flame the gift of God he had received when Paul had laid his hands on him. He then added that the Spirit given to us by God does not make us timid but gives us power, love, and self-discipline (2 Timothy 1: 6-7).

The encouragement that Barnabas brought to the church in Antioch did not consist merely of words. Words are important and can have impact, but Barnabas also looked for ways to actively fan into greater flame all that God was doing. He immediately went to work to help train up pastors and leaders who could further direct the church and steward the Holy Spirit's ministry that was taking place so that the outreach of the church might become more effective. First, he traveled approximately 100 miles to track down and recruit Saul of Tarsus. Saul, who would later be called Paul, was well trained in the Scriptures and had dramatically encountered Jesus while on the road to persecute believers in Damascus. Not only was Saul a former Jewish Pharisee who had been radically transformed by the Spirit of God, he was also specifically called to bring the

Gospel to the Gentiles. In his very being, he personified what God was doing by His Spirit in Antioch. Together, Barnabas and Saul then continued to meet with the church and teach them. At this point, the believers began to take on their own name change. Joseph, who had become Barnabas, and Saul, who would become Paul, were pastoring the Antiochian believers, who began to be called Christians.

Barnabas and Saul were not the only leaders of the church in Antioch. Prophets also came from Jerusalem to serve the growing church. By telling us about these prophets, the Bible is letting us know that ongoing, Spirit-empowered ministry was still taking place as the church developed and matured. Spiritual gifts continued to flow among the believers. In fact, Agabus understood and prophesied by the Spirit that a severe famine would spread over the entire Roman empire. Why would God reveal this to the young church? It was not to impress anyone with how great of a prophet Agabus apparently was. It was not a demonstration of the height of his spirituality, nor was it intended to cause anyone to therefore be in awe of the scope of the prophetic word he brought. The point, rather, was to embolden the believers to greater service and sacrifice on behalf of those in need. Just as the earlier believers in Jerusalem had worked to bring significant help to those among them who were in need after the outpouring at Pentecost, God also worked in the aftermath of the outpouring of His Spirit in Antioch to similarly show His love through the unity of the Jewish and Gentile believers and their joint efforts to bless, encourage, and literally feed the Judean believers who were being impacted by the famine. This example demonstrates how the move of the Spirit in the church of Antioch worked over time through careful teaching and ministry from empowered leadership to help all the believers mature in their faith and to engage in acts of loving service!

Four to five years later, as we move on to chapter 13 in the book of Acts, we discover that the leadership team of this church had expanded again. There were multiple prophets and teachers now serving in the ministry of the Spirit in Antioch, including Barnabas, Simeon, Lucius, Manaen, and Saul. The titles of these leaders, "prophets" and "teachers," show us that there was a clear intersection and cooperation between biblical teaching and charismatic gifts. The backgrounds of these leaders demonstrate they represented a wonderful cross-section of both Jews and Gentiles. Their places of origin showcase ethnic diversity. Their social status reflected both the low and high. Over the intervening years, the expansion of this leadership team suggests that there had been an intentional raising up, establishment of, and appointing of Spirit-empowered leaders to advance the work of the ministry in the church. Acts 13:2 tells us that they were all engaged in spiritual discipline and joint worship: *"While they were worshiping the Lord and fasting, the Holy Spirit said, . . ."* Having experienced the move of the Spirit time and again, they continued to make space to practice the presence of the Lord, allowing opportunity for them to connect with His supernatural voice. As they did, the Spirit gave them added direction: *"'Set aside Barnabas and Saul for the work to which I have called them.'"* We are clearly meant to see that the ongoing ministry of spiritual gifts, and especially the gift of prophecy, not only continued to flow in the life of the church but also continued to ultimately serve the spread of the Gospel. The message of salvation through Jesus remained their overriding priority! After hearing from God, the leadership laid their hands on the two newly appointed missionaries in prayer and sent them off for this very purpose. In a similar way, we must deeply internalize the inherent ongoing connection between the supernatural workings of the Spirit and the spread of the Gospel message to those in need.

LESSONS FOR THE CHURCH TODAY

As the Gospel message spread from Jerusalem to Antioch, it is apparent that the Lord worked through the leadership to ensure that the ministry of the Holy Spirit remained purposely intertwined with the mission to share the Good News of Jesus. The ministry of the Spirit in Samaria had not been haphazard or accidental. Peter and John picked up where Philip had left off to ensure that the new believers there were walking in their own ongoing experience of the Holy Spirit's ministry. God had worked through Philip to perform great signs and miracles while he was among them, but the fact remained that the ministry of the Spirit was not intended to be reserved just for those called to vocational ministry. The Old Testament prophet Joel had long ago proclaimed that the Lord would pour out His Spirit *"on all flesh."* Peter and John did not leave Samaria before intentionally helping the believers discover and embrace the baptism in the Spirit for themselves. The baptism in the Holy Spirit and the ongoing supernatural ministry of the Spirit through the lives of the believers were meant to enable the continued proclamation of the Gospel. We have every reason to believe that this remains the intent of God even now.

In Antioch, we see a similar focus in the leadership of the church there. People were turning to the Lord in great numbers from both Jewish and Gentile populations. This work of evangelism was now coming through numerous other believers and not just the original apostles as these new believers moved into the region. Yet the church leadership from Jerusalem also found ways to intentionally encourage, bless, support, and give shape to what the Spirit was doing as the inhabitants of Antioch surrendered to the lordship of Jesus. The Jerusalem leaders sent Barnabas. Barnabas recruited Saul. Additional prophets arrived to help. For the next several years, the expanding group of believers were taught, discipled, and strengthened in their walk with God. Five years later, the leadership then consisted of both prophets and teachers who practiced the presence of God as a matter of discipline, and they remained as committed as ever to the spread of the Gospel beyond their community.

Chapter 5, "Embracing the Move of the Spirit," helped us to see that churches who thrive in the Spirit must at all times be motivated to minister in the same love that God has for each and every person on the planet. Without love it all comes to naught. This chapter has endeavored to remind us that the central content of that loving ministry must be the proclamation of the Gospel message of Jesus with the corresponding empowerment of believers by the Holy Spirit. One aspect should not be emphasized to the minimization or exclusion of the other. Both elements are meant to flow together. It is the responsibility of leadership to be intentional about proclaiming the message of Jesus and then to teach the believers to do the same. It is also the equal responsibility of leadership to actively proclaim the ministry of the Holy Spirit and to make a place for ongoing growth, experience, and deployment of spiritual gifts among the members of the church body. The supernatural move of the Spirit is to be anticipated and embraced in service to the furtherance of the Gospel.

Numerous churches today long for "revival." Though we may all have expressed the desire to see such an outpouring in our individual churches, has this hope gotten mired in the muck of mere passive wishing? What if we intentionally worked to continually fan into flame the work of the Spirit by renewing an emphasis on reaching the lost with the message of Jesus and by empowering believers by the ministry of the Holy Spirit? How might it look to actively expect, plan for, and deliberately pursue this vision in your setting? Where this two-pronged mission becomes the church's primary passion, the possibilities of what the Lord might do to bring transformation to a community become limitless. In order to better explore the wonders of these possibilities, and as we look to find ways of making a place for them in our churches, we should now examine the powerful move of the Spirit in another church found in the book of Acts. Ephesus, here we come!

PAUSE AND REFLECT:

- It was in Antioch that the believers were first called "**Christians**," or literally, "**little Christs**." What is the reputation of your church? How is it known in your community? How do first-time visitors respond to what they experience? How does that reputation match both your church's calling and mission?

- How does the surprising unity between the Jewish and Gentile believers compare with the unity among the members of your church? Are there divisions that interfere with the effective ministry of the Gospel or the supernatural ministry of the Spirit? What steps could you take to help foster greater unity?

- How intentional is your church about sharing the Gospel with those who have not yet embraced Jesus as Lord? How does this look in your gatherings? How does this look during the time between meetings? How are believers taught and encouraged to share their faith?

- How intentional is your church about presenting and emphasizing the baptism in the Holy Spirit? In what ways are the gifts of the Spirit practiced in the life of the church? What might it look like to utilize outside help to bring encouragement and instruction? How are believers taught and encouraged to participate in the ministry of the Holy Spirit?

- In Acts 13, the leaders of the church in Antioch practiced spiritual disciplines (such as fasting) together. They spent time worshiping the Lord together. How does your leadership team (staff, elders, key leaders, etc.) practice the presence of the Lord together? What room is there for regularly gathering as a leadership team to seek the Lord and to listen for the voice of the Spirit? What could this look like in future days?

Chapter 7
Growing in our Experience of the Spirit: *The Church in Ephesus*

Before taking a deeper look at the next portion in our Acts overview, let's consider a contemporary analogy from the world of astronomy. In April of 1990, the Hubble Space Telescope was launched into orbit. Since that time, astrophysicists have declared that the discoveries assisted by that orbital telescope have revolutionized humanity's understanding of the universe. Among the startling observations are the unexpected finding of multiple new moons and extrasolar planets, the verifying of the rate of the universe's expansion, and the revelation that essentially every galaxy is formed around a central black hole in space. These findings and more have all contributed to major advancements in the scientific exploration of the cosmos.

Thirty-one years after Hubble was first put to use, the state-of-the-art James Webb Space Telescope (JWST) was also deployed into space during December of 2021. Its larger size and new infrared technology enable it to look at the same sections of deep space first seen via Hubble with exponentially greater clarity and detail. In fact, within mere days of first coming online, it began detecting thousands of new galaxies at distances far beyond anything we had previously been able to measure. It took vast sections of the night sky and provided insight and information beyond what we previously knew to even be possible. While Hubble helped us to find the existence of new planets far beyond our solar system, the JWST has enabled the study of the atmospheric conditions of those same worlds. In other words, the JWST has allowed scientists to explore the universe in ways far greater than anything that has come before. Previously we had a certain level of information about the universe, but we had insufficient data to anticipate what might still be learned or to understand what might yet lay out there waiting to be discovered. Simply, we didn't know what we didn't know! Today, the JWST has opened our eyes to all sorts of new possibilities. It has enabled us to see, dream, study, and advance in ways we did not expect, and it seems we are just getting started as this new work of exploration is unfolding. Scientists have never been more thrilled at the prospects to come.

As the book of Acts unfolds, there seems to be a similar exponential advancement concerning the work of the Holy Spirit and His movement through the believers. This progress points the reader to greater and greater expectation and understanding, enabling ministry far beyond what the first believers initially anticipated. With the outpouring of the Holy Spirit on the day of Pentecost came power and authority that enabled the effective witness of Christ and His message by those who believed. Prophetic utterances, healing of the sick and infirm, speaking in tongues, and numerous other gifts and displays of the Spirit all had tremendous impact as the followers of Christ continued to proclaim the Gospel everywhere they went. The baptism in the Holy Spirit had undeniably empowered the Church to touch others with creative power that transformed the body as well as the soul.

The move of God in this way was nothing short of amazing. Yet, the outpouring of the Holy Spirit that took place in Ephesus (as found in Acts 19) was unlike anything that had come before. Such a statement is not intended to minimize the powerful and amazing impact that the Spirit had already accomplished in the advancement of the Church or to inadvertently make light of the incredible transformation that had transpired in the lives of thousands of individuals as the message of the Gospel spread through the believers. However, it seems in many ways that the supernatural move of the Spirit that had taken place in the first eighteen chapters was just the "warmup" when compared to the powerful display that came about over time in the church in Ephesus. When we study the Scriptures and take a closer look at what God did by His Spirit in Ephesus, we can be awakened to the realization that there is so much more to learn and experience. We can begin to understand that the possibilities of what God may want to supernaturally accomplish through His Church are limitless.

As we cooperate with the Spirit of God and as we believe He can certainly work through us to bring substantive and loving transformation to others, do we anticipate that there are even greater works yet to come? After all, Jesus told His disciples during His last supper with them, *"I tell you the truth, anyone who has faith in me will do what I have been doing. He will do even greater things than these, because I am going to the Father"* (John 14:12). How could this even be feasible? Just four verses later, Jesus revealed how by saying, *"And I will ask the Father, and he will give you another Counselor to be with you forever — the Spirit of truth. The world cannot accept him, because it neither sees him nor knows him. But you know him, for he lives with you and will be in you"* (John 14:16-17). Great and even greater works are possible because of the Holy Spirit living in us! Do we genuinely believe this? Are we hungry for such a move of God's Spirit? Do we yearn for it?

THE BEGINNING OF MINISTRY IN EPHESUS

Near the end of his second missionary journey, Paul stopped briefly in Ephesus (Acts 18:19). Ephesus was the fourth most populous city in the Roman empire (behind Rome, Alexandria, and Antioch), and it was the key harbor for the entire province of Asia. As such, it was a strategic location for communication and a hub for all the major trade routes. What happened in Ephesus could potentially touch the entire region.

Paul's initial visit to Ephesus was incredibly short, lasting perhaps less than a week. He was there just long enough to minister in the synagogue, where he spent his time reasoning with the Jews. Though they asked him to stay longer, he declined because he had a ship to catch. He was determined to continue to Jerusalem by way of Caesarea and then return to Antioch where he first started. He did, however, promise to come back to Ephesus later, God willing. On the other hand, his traveling companions, Priscilla and Aquila, stayed in Ephesus and continued to minister the Gospel. Soon afterward Apollos, a Jew from Alexandria, also arrived and began preaching in the Ephesian synagogue himself. The Scripture is quite clear in its description of Apollos. *"He was a learned man, with a thorough knowledge of the Scriptures. He had been instructed in the way of the Lord, and he spoke with great fervor and taught about Jesus accurately, though he knew only the baptism of John"* (Acts 18:24-25). What seems apparent is that Apollos understood the basic tenets of the Gospel message and was able to present them well. However, something was lacking. When Priscilla and Aquila heard Apollos preach, they opened their home to him but also *"explained to him the way of God more adequately"* (Acts 18:26). From this reading, the teaching of Apollos was correct as far as it went. He was not presenting anything false or in error but rather needed a more complete message. We don't have the privilege of knowing exactly what was taught to Apollos by Priscilla and Aquila, but we do know that when he left Ephesus and went on to the region of Achaia, he was able to minister there with great effectiveness, *"for he vigorously refuted the Jews in public debate, proving from the Scriptures that Jesus was the Christ"* (Acts 18:28).

Biblical scholars have long wondered exactly what the missing component was in Apollos's ministry before his encounter with Priscilla and Aquila. He apparently understood well the Gospel because Luke comments that he was *"instructed in the way of the Lord"* and that he *"taught about Jesus accurately."* These phrases suggest to us that he certainly understood who Jesus was, why He came into the world, the significance of His death and resurrection, and the importance of personally embracing Christ as

> **PAUSE AND REFLECT:**
>
> - Consider the level of anticipation and expectancy regarding the move of the Spirit among the members and the leadership of your local church. Is there a sense of vibrant life, or are people simply tired and weary? What aspects of the Lord's ministry in your church could use a sharper focus?
>
> - If Priscilla and Aquila could observe the ministry taking place in your church, what would they find? Is there a regular calling for people to turn from sin and turn to the Lord? Is the Gospel message of Jesus a central focus of the preaching? Do people have the opportunity to experience baptism in water as part of their conversion to Christ? Is there also emphasis on the baptism in the Holy Spirit and living by the Spirit's power?
>
> - If you were to make changes in any of these areas, where would you start? Would extended times of prayer and seeking the Lord together with your staff and leaders be helpful? Does there need to be some further instruction so that the way of the Spirit can be understood more adequately? What other steps could you take?

Lord. What, then, was inadequate about the preaching of Apollos? The biggest clue we have is in the statement, *"he knew only the baptism of John."* John the Baptist baptized people as part of their heartfelt repentance from sin. The baptism he offered was the opportunity to embrace a new life before God as people prepared themselves for the coming of the Messiah. This is all good and right, so what else could be needed?

Some theologians suggest that what could have been lacking in the ministry of Apollos was the opportunity for Christian baptism as people called on Jesus as Lord. Christian baptism was seen as a step beyond the baptism of John because of its identification with the death, burial, and resurrection of Jesus and the understanding that those who come into Christ become new creations with renewed hearts and fresh starts. Many others, however, also point to the need for an emphasis on the baptism in the Holy Spirit. In fact, the events of the following chapter, Acts 19, seem to be an illustration of this very idea! Either way, the preaching of Apollos while he was in Ephesus can be likened to the images taken by the Hubble Space Telescope. What was presented by him was accurate and revolutionary. It was like nothing the people had heard or seen before, and it brought enlightenment and transformation. Yet there was so much more to be discovered and experienced. Just as the new James Webb Space Telescope has made our previous views of the heavens so much sharper and allowed for greater depths of understanding, the outpouring of the Spirit is meant to similarly expand our experience of just how much more there is to know and embrace as we learn to live (and even thrive) in the Spirit.

THE EXPLOSIVE GROWTH OF THE MOVE OF THE SPIRIT

As Paul began his third missionary journey, he soon returned to Ephesus and found about twelve disciples (Acts 19:1-7). However, he also quickly discovered that these disciples had not received the Holy Spirit when they believed. Moreover, they had not even heard that there was a Holy Spirit. The baptism they had received was John's baptism, the baptism of repentance. The state of their understanding makes us wonder if they had responded to the ministry of Apollos with great vigor but were ultimately left lacking in their experience in the same way that perhaps he had been. Paul brought immediate correction by doing two things. First, he baptized them in the name of the Lord Jesus. Second, he placed his hands on them and the Holy Spirit came upon them. The impact of the infilling of the Spirit was immediate as the disciples each spoke in tongues and prophesied. It is important to note that this outpouring of the Spirit was not the culmination of Paul's ministry in Ephesus, but rather just the beginning.

For the next three months Paul continued to minister in the synagogue, speaking boldly and persuasively about the kingdom of God. When some of the synagogue members eventually became obstinate and divisive, Paul shifted his ministry to the lecture hall of Tyrannus where he led daily discussions as he continued to tutor the growing group of believers. This arrangement went on for an additional two years. The number of disciples increased, the Spirit of God continued to move in powerful ways, and active discussions took place every day as the believers grew in the faith. The result was that all the Jews and Greeks throughout the province of Asia heard the Word of the Lord. How did this happen? It was not simply achieved by Paul's efforts. Rather, it seems that the believers who were trained in the daily sessions in Ephesus then traveled across the region, effectively ministering the Gospel! What a wonderful and convincing example of the unity between the supernatural ministry of the Spirit and the ongoing proclamation of the Word through the followers of Jesus! Such is the hope of every church body. Yet, this was not all that God was doing. The supernatural work of the Spirit kept increasing.

Acts 19:11 also tells us that *"God did extraordinary miracles through Paul."* It is worth examining the exact word order found in the original Greek text. Translated word for word in order, the sentence reads, "Miracles then, *not being ordinary,* God was performing by the hands of Paul." What a fascinating idea! Among the categorizations of the types of miracles that God works by His Spirit, there are apparently "ordinary" miracles and "not ordinary" (or "extraordinary") miracles! The text goes on to give examples as it begins to discuss works of healing.

Throughout the book of Acts supernatural works of healing were commonly associated with the work of the Spirit and the proclamation of Jesus. Healing was a widespread and serious need in every community. In fact, it has been reported that in all major cities worldwide from the time of antiquity until the late 1800s, the death rate of those born in the city exceeded the corresponding birth rates. Sickness and disease tended to run rampant everywhere. The proclamation of the kingdom of God, however, included a declaration of healing for those in need, and stories of healing are found throughout the book of Acts in accordance with the growth of the early Church. In chapter 3, Peter took hold of the hand of a lame man near the temple and told him to rise and walk in the name of Jesus. Instantly, the man was healed! In chapter 5, sick people were laid out in the streets so that at least Peter's shadow might fall on them, and they were healed! In chapter 8, many who were paralyzed and lame were healed through the ministry of Philip. In chapter 9, a paralyzed man named Aeneas, who had been bedridden for eight years, was completely healed as Peter announced, *"'Jesus Christ heals you. Get up and take care of your mat'"* (Acts 9:34). In Acts 14, Paul told a crippled man, *"'Stand up on your feet'"* (verse 10), and the man jumped up straightaway. What powerful and wondrous works each of these healings were! It is perhaps even more wondrous to realize that such works could be considered "ordinary" miracles.

In Ephesus, the miraculous healing work of the Spirit increased in astounding ways. Even simple handkerchiefs and aprons that had merely come into contact with Paul were then taken to the sick with astonishing results. With the arrival of these cloths, illnesses were absolutely cured and people were delivered of demonic spirits even though Paul was not physically present. Can you imagine the surprise, joy, and excitement that must have flooded the community as this happened not once, but time after time, in numerous situations?

In addition to these miraculous healings, a great awe began to fall upon the people of Ephesus as the name of Jesus was held in high esteem. Some, however, tried to use the message of Jesus for their own gain, and a confrontation between seven sons of a Jewish priest named Sceva and a demoniac did not go so well. These seven sons were trying to minister deliverance to the demonized man in the name of Jesus, but they had not yet become believers in Jesus themselves, and they were not filled with the Spirit. They were trying to use the name of Jesus like a magic incantation, and it did not work. Instead, the demon-possessed man overpowered them all and beat them severely. The message began to spread: the message of Jesus was serious business and demanded an honest, heartfelt response. Many began to repent of their sinful actions. Those who had practiced sorcery publicly burned their scrolls and spell books. Acts 19:20 tells us, *"In this way the word of the Lord spread widely and grew in power."*

By the time Paul was preparing to leave Ephesus and journey on to Jerusalem, close to three years had transpired. It was the longest period that he had ministered in any one place since he first set out from Antioch on his initial missionary endeavors. What God did in the city of Ephesus during that time was nothing less than astounding. From powerful and unusual miracles to moments of mass repentance among the inhabitants to the spread of the Gospel throughout the entire province, the Spirit of God was moving forcefully . . . and wonderfully. What God did then, He is still in the business of doing today. God is yet looking to touch each generation with the message of Christ in the power of the Spirit. The Lord's work in Ephesus reminds us that there is more to both expect and experience as we remain faithful to minister as He directs. What surprises might He yet have in store?

MAKING SPACE FOR THE MINISTRY OF THE SPIRIT

Paul's ministry in Ephesus presents a powerful series of lessons for the contemporary Church if we are willing to acknowledge them. First, the proclamation of the message of Christ is incomplete if it does not include the active reception of the baptism in the Holy Spirit. Apollos knew of John's baptism, but Priscilla and Aquila helped him understand that this was an incomplete message by itself. The disciples that Paul encountered on his return visit to Ephesus also knew only the importance of repentance but did not understand the necessity of being filled with the Spirit of God. Paul used that area of need as the starting point of his ministry and ended up laying his hands on the Ephesian disciples to receive the Holy Spirit. The infilling and continuing ministry of the Spirit are meant to take a central role in the life of the individual believer while becoming a defining factor in the messaging, experience, and outreach of the larger Church.

Second, the move of the Spirit in Ephesus invites us to believe and press for more. Not only did miracles take place there, but they also turned out to be extraordinary ones! Not only did people come to Christ, but there was public confession of sins, followed by great acts of demonstrable contrition! Not only was a church established, but the entire region was also exposed to the Gospel message of Jesus! The Word of God spread everywhere! Do we believe this is possible today, or have we settled for the idea that this was meant to happen only in biblical settings long ago? Sometimes people can labor for the Gospel for so long in a particular area that they give up hope that God might move in such an impactful way. Paul's message in chapter 6 of his letter to the Galatian church provides encouragement for just such a moment: *"Let us not become weary in doing good, for at the proper time we will reap a harvest if we do not give up"* (Galatians 6:9). History has shown this to be undeniably true. Countless stories of repentance, renewal, revival, and even reformation have persisted through the ages, from days of old right through to our current times. God still saves, still forgives, still restores, still transforms, still heals, still delivers, and still works mighty wonders wherever people are faithful to proclaim the Gospel and live by the power and character of the Holy Spirit. If you are yearning for more of this work of the Spirit, more is certainly possible.

A third lesson evidenced by Paul's ministry in Ephesus is the importance of determined, intentional, ongoing discipleship. It is perhaps both inspiring and intimidating to read that the disciples met daily for discussion in the lecture hall of Tyrannus. They found a place to meet regularly and often as they sought to apply the Word of God and the ministry of the Spirit to daily living. While no one should begin thinking there is some kind of magic formula that somehow equates to "meet this many times together and you will see an explosive move of the Spirit," it nevertheless seems apparent that the church in Ephesus was determined to make space to learn, grow, develop, and mature as believers in Christ and as ministers of the Gospel. They did not just talk about the ministry of the Spirit; they practiced His presence. They held on to the importance of being filled with the Holy Spirit and actively worked to touch others with His presence and power.

The writer of Hebrews tells us that *"Jesus Christ is the same yesterday and today and forever"* (13:8). The statement is made in the broader context of a call to deeply consider the way of life that was engaged by the Church leaders who have come before us and to then imitate their faith (verse 7). As these original disciples were filled with the Spirit and used greatly to minister the Gospel and advance the kingdom of God, so too God is looking to work through people today. Jesus has not changed. His mission is still to seek and save those who are lost. The Church serves in a very real sense as His hands and feet to touch others with His presence and power and to go to wherever people can be found so that all might be saved. There is so much more that He will yet do. Do we have faith to believe and persevere? The move of the Spirit will grow in surprising ways for those who keep their focus on Christ Jesus!

PAUSE AND REFLECT:

- How would you describe the balance between practical teaching, discipleship, and Spirit-empowered ministry in the church of Ephesus? How does that compare with the experience of your church? Is one aspect weaker than the other? What would it take to better develop that area?

- What most inspires you about the Spirit's work in Ephesus? In what ways would you like to see the Holy Spirit touch others through the members of your church today? How can you cast that ministry vision for others to see as well?

- What was the focus of Paul's message and ministry in Ephesus? What does that answer suggest to us about the focus that God intends for our current setting?

- Would you say that the miraculous healings and deliverances taking place in Ephesus were the "center" of the Spirit's work in Ephesus or the "byproduct" of His work? What is the difference? What lessons can we learn from that?

- In what ways does your church make deliberate space for the ministry of the Spirit? How might creating that space increase anticipation and expectation for an increased work of the Spirit in your community?

Chapter 8
Guidelines for Spirit-Empowered Ministry *(The Church in Corinth)*

Have you ever heard the expression "looking through rose-colored lenses"? It originated during the time of the U.S. Civil War. Though eyeglasses first came into use during the thirteenth century and became popularized during the seventeenth century, the development of sunglasses did not transpire until around 1800. Even then, it was the U.S. Civil War that first put them to great practical use. First, they became standard issue for both sharpshooters and artillerymen, helping them to zero in on their targets despite the brightness of the sun. These glasses often utilized blue, violet, or even green lenses as a defense against the bright daylight. However, it was soon discovered by medical officers in the field that a change to pink lenses could have a significant impact on the overall morale of the soldiers. The Civil War was the bloodiest war in American history. The total number of Americans who were killed equaled nearly as many as all other U.S. wars combined right through to today. These massive casualties resulted in significant psychological trauma to troops from both sides. In an effort to better prevent that trauma, many medics recommended the use of glasses with pink-colored lenses. Something about how these lenses filtered light was believed to be a valid treatment for depression. This led to the rise of the phrase "looking through rose-colored lenses." The phrase eventually evolved to describe a decision to filter out the negative or hard aspects of life while remembering only the positive qualities in an attempt to hold on to a peaceful and joyful disposition. In the end, however, the prescription of rose lenses proved to be woefully ineffective. Suffering soldiers had to find other ways to come to terms with the harsh realities of their experiences and enter into recovery.

When we read the Scriptural accounts of the early Church, we can have a similar tendency to hold on to "rose-colored lenses." In our eagerness to celebrate and emulate all the good that was taking place, we can inadvertently become blind to the problem spots that were also occurring. The movement of the Spirit in the development of the Church throughout the book of Acts is fascinating to behold. The early Church was teeming with experiences of the power and presence of the Holy Spirit. The growth of the kingdom of God in the Church in Jerusalem, followed by its expansion to Antioch and then to numerous places beyond, inspires us and contributes to the heart cry of many in the Church today: "Do it again, Lord!" Yet, it is also important to understand that there were crisis moments and problems that also had to be addressed in the life of the Church over time.

While the Spirit is always perfect, how we cooperate, interact, and endeavor to flow along with Him is not always so perfect. Despite being the redeemed of the Lord, being filled with the Spirit, and committing ourselves to follow in the steps of Christ, none of us is fully complete yet. We are learning, growing, and maturing, which means we can and do make mistakes along the way. We are led astray when we misunderstand our experiences, when we succumb to the influence and temptations of our flesh, and when we simply get caught up in the exuberance of all that God may be doing without simultaneously holding on to the wisdom and guidance He also offers. It can be hard to be truly honest about these tendencies. Often we would rather look at all that happens in the ministry of a church through rose-colored spiritual lenses. We must instead be willing to probe deeper and press in for what is authentic and honest if we desire to truly thrive in our relationship with the Spirit of God. This requires that we continually choose to stay humble and teachable as we journey with the Lord and that we remain ever ready to engage in scrutiny and correction along the way. To better explore such concepts, let's look at another key New Testament church: Corinth.

OFF TO A GREAT START
According to the book of Acts, before the incredible outpouring of the Spirit and

all the miraculous ministry that took place in Ephesus, Paul had first ministered in Corinth. Corinth was the capital city of Achaea. As such, it was a major urban center in the heart of Greek culture. It had also been resettled by the Romans during the expansion of the Empire. Thus, the city reflected the pagan influence of both groups. In the time of Paul, Corinth had become renowned for both its affluence and its decadence.

After arriving in Corinth, Paul met the husband-and-wife team, Priscilla and Aquila. He ended up working alongside them as a tentmaker to support himself while living there. Every Sabbath he would minister in the synagogue, bringing the Gospel to both the Jews and the God-fearing Greeks. Before long, Silas and Timothy arrived, and he was then able to devote himself full time to preaching as he proclaimed Jesus as the Messiah. However, the Jews came out against him, and he ended up changing tactics, focusing his efforts primarily on reaching the Gentiles. Soon many began to come into the kingdom of God as they put their trust in Jesus and were baptized. The church in Corinth was born in spite of persistent opposition! The Lord greatly encouraged Paul by assuring him supernaturally in a dream that He would keep him safe, so Paul stayed in Corinth for a year and a half teaching the Word of God. Eventually civil unrest came to a head as the Jews united in their opposition against Paul and brought charges against him. However, the Roman proconsul sided with Paul, and the crowd turned against the synagogue leader. Paul was protected, just as the Spirit had revealed. After a time, Paul and his companions traveled on, but the church in Corinth continued to grow. There was much to celebrate as the kingdom of God advanced and increased in Corinth, just as when the move of the Spirit had made tremendous impact in other places.

PROBLEMS AND QUESTIONS ARISE

The Holy Spirit was certainly ministering powerfully in Corinth, but that does not mean all was therefore healthy and right in that growing local church. In fact, while Paul was later ministering in Ephesus (and even as extraordinary miracles were happening over the course of his three years there), he ended up writing a letter filled with important corrections for the church in Corinth. In the first chapter he addressed problems of disunity and factions among the believers. They were becoming divided as they played favorites among the various leaders who had ministered there, including Paul, Apollos, and Peter (called Cephas).

Some even tried to show how spiritual they were by proclaiming, "I follow Christ!" (1 Corinthians 1:12), with likely emphasis on the all-important "I." In chapter 5, Paul confronted sexual sin among certain members of the church, and he warned the believers that they too would be defiled if they remained unwilling to take the same stance as he did against that sin. To follow Christ is to simultaneously say no to sin, and Paul was quick to admonish the Church to take decisive action to set things right (1 Corinthians 5:9-13). He went on in chapter six to address all kinds of additional sins, reminding the Corinthians that they had been washed and justified in the name of Jesus by the Spirit of God when they believed and were therefore equipped to live a life free of such entanglements (1 Corinthians 6:9-11). He also reminded them that their individual bodies were temples of the Holy Spirit and that they had all been bought at a steep price; therefore, they had an obligation to honor God with their bodies (1 Corinthians 6:19-20).

After addressing these issues of holiness and integrity, Paul then addressed a series of questions that had arisen in the Church. He offered guidelines for marriage as well as considerations for various other situations and stations of life (chapter 7). In chapter 8, he discussed what do to with food sold in the market that had previously been sacrificed to

> **PAUSE AND REFLECT:**
>
> - How hard is it to have an honest discussion with your leaders about issues in your church? Is there a tendency to only look at the ministry of the church through rose-colored glasses? What would help enable a more transparent and helpful conversation?
>
> - If Paul were to write a letter to your church, what issues might he want to address? Is the church unified or divided? Are there active issues of sin that are being conveniently ignored? Is there a need for corrective action? How might God want to address this? What changes should be considered?
>
> - Some of the issues that Paul addressed in the first part of his letter to the Corinthians were corporate issues that impact the whole body of believers. Others had more of an individual focus. What does the Holy Spirit want to say to you individually regarding standards of sin and holiness in your life? How can you help your leadership and staff listen to hear and then deeply consider what the Spirit may want to say to them? What about the entire church?

idols (remember that Corinth was a pagan city!). In chapter 10, he shared that the embrace of sin brings incalculable destruction and harm and that no one should think they are above temptation. However, he also wrote that in every potential adverse situation, God does provide a way to escape and overcome (1 Corinthians 10:13). In chapter 11, Paul began to address concerns that had developed regarding the move of the Spirit, but by the time he got to this issue in the letter, he had well reaffirmed standards of personal holiness across numerous categories and issues within the church.

Taking such great lengths to address these issues in the church serves to remind us even today that while we may greatly desire to move into a deeper experience of the supernatural workings of the Spirit of God, we cannot afford to be apathetic toward our own sinful temptations or to become divisive and quarrelsome with other believers. God has called us to a higher standard, and we should not think that any of us can thrive in our relationship with the Spirit of God if we are simultaneously lax in our commitment and devotion to the directives of the Word. Moreover, in his opening to his letter to the believers in Rome, Paul refers to the Spirit as *"the Spirit of holiness"* (Romans 1:4). Throughout the Scripture, He is not just the Spirit. He is the *Holy Spirit*. This truth cannot be conveniently ignored or dismissed by any of us.

GUIDELINES FOR SPIRIT MINISTRY

Have you ever been tempted to drink water from a garden hose? The problem with this is that a garden hose is not necessarily designed to carry water for human consumption; it is designed to carry water to a garden (obviously!). We do not generally think about the cleanliness of the hose. It is typically left outside where it can easily pick up dirt, mold, and other contaminants. The water it conducts may be pure at its source, but as it passes through the hose it can become tainted. Who ever thinks to occasionally scrub out the inside? No one! This generally has no bearing on the plants that receive the water, but for people who opt to drink from it, the taste of the water from the hose can become quite abhorrent!

The move of the Spirit through people will likely take on the flavor and personality of those individuals. This is not necessarily bad. The New Testament contains four written Gospels, and each one gives us a bit of fresh perspective and insight as God brings the message through four unique writers. The challenge in Christian ministry is how to serve as a pure conduit for the presence and power of the Holy Spirit without unduly and negatively impacting the outcome of that ministry through poor character, indifference toward sin, unnecessary habits and traditions, or other unfortunate practices that contribute to error and confusion. How many times have people been turned away from the Gospel because of the unloving actions and behaviors of its messengers? How often have powerful revival movements in history gone awry because of a lack of careful review of or ongoing submission to biblical instruction and standards?

The book of Acts on its own does not give us any specific details about the active, ongoing work of the Holy Spirit in Corinth, especially as it concerns descriptions of supernatural events and activity in the life of the Church. It does, however, present us with the most important impact of the ministry: many people believed and were baptized! However, chapters 12, 13, and 14 of Paul's first letter to the Corinthians make it clear that the supernatural flow of the Spirit of God through the members of that church was indeed a vibrant part of the ministry there. To be fair, a full analysis of these chapters is simply too large a task for this book, and yet clear guidelines do stand out as we read these verses. In our zeal to pursue the supernatural ministry of the Spirit in the Church today, we can sometimes forget that the Scriptures provide us with constructive guidelines and directives concerning charismatic gifts and the engagement of supernatural activity. If we intend for our churches to truly become conduits for the powerful display of the Spirit's ministry in the loving advance of the kingdom of God and the effective spread of the message of Jesus, it is appropriate that we become familiar with these guidelines and actively apply them. None of us wants the ministry of the Spirit to become unduly tainted or negatively impacted by our poor practices and habits. We must be willing to do the arduous work of self-evaluation and then submit ourselves to the Word. With that in mind, let's consider eight biblical truths/guidelines derived from the teachings of 1 Corinthians 12-14 and ask ourselves some practical application questions along the way.

1. God wants us to be well informed about Spirit-empowered ministry. The Church needs to be actively engaged in teaching about the move of the Spirit and the use of spiritual gifts. *"Now about the gifts of the Spirit, brothers and sisters, I do not want you to be ignorant"*

(1 Corinthians 12:1). Paul writes chapters 12-14 in response to questions he has received from the Corinthian church. It is a lengthy discussion of the ministry of the Holy Spirit and the spiritual gifts He provides to empower the Church. Right from the start, we can see that the ministry of the Spirit is meant to be accompanied by thorough, ongoing teaching that keeps the Church informed and engaged. What does this look like in the current ministry of your church? Are there ways that the ministry of the Spirit and the implementation of spiritual gifts could be better addressed and presented?

2. **Though spiritual gifts can be diverse and empower all kinds of Christian service, they are workings of the Spirit and do not belong to any individual.** *"There are different kinds of gifts, but the same Spirit. There are different kinds of service, but the same Lord. There are different kinds of working, but the same God works all of them in all men"* (1 Corinthians 12:4-6). The deployment of spiritual gifts and other activities of the Spirit are meant to point others back to God. They are not demonstrations of the piety or greatness of any individual and must never become a source of pride. All glory must go to God! How do the members of your church perceive those who operate in spiritual gifts? Are they placed on proverbial pedestals in the collective mind of the believers? Is there an understanding and expectation that the Spirit of God may want to actively work through any and all of the believers? How could this humble mindset better permeate the culture of your church?

3. **The Spirit of God is expressed in the life of the Church for the collective benefit of others.** *"Now to each one the manifestation of the Spirit is given for the common good"* (1 Corinthians 12:7). In this verse we should notice the Lord's intention to bring the kingdom of God to those in need. This is exactly what occurred during the earthly ministry of Jesus. Peter proclaimed in Acts 10:37-38, *"You know what has happened throughout Judea, beginning in Galilee after the baptism that John preached – how God anointed Jesus of Nazareth with the Holy Spirit and power, and how He went around doing good and healing all who were under the power of the devil, because God was with Him."* This is still what the Spirit of God wants to do as Jesus continues to minister through the individual members who comprise the church today. Moreover, the words

"common good" take on a new dimension when we consider the original Greek language in which Paul wrote his letter to the Corinthians. The phrase is a translation of the single word, **συμφέρον** *(sympheron)*, which means "to heap together for someone else's benefit." It shares the same root as the word "symphony," which creates a wonderful word picture for us. In the same way that a great piece of music can powerfully move an entire audience with the many instrumentalists combining their individual parts in concert with one another, the Greek word suggests a greater good is served when we each embrace and deploy the spiritual gifts the Spirit has given us with the same shared single goal: the advancement of the kingdom of God in the lives of people for the purposes of rescue and redemption. How does your church help each member to understand that the Spirit of God wants to deploy spiritual gifts through them? How are those members given opportunity to utilize their spiritual gifts? How are they guided, taught, corrected, and encouraged? What is the "common good" that the Spirit wants to bring about through the ministry of your church?

4. **It is appropriate and right to eagerly desire spiritual gifts, especially those that will be of the most benefit to others.** *"But eagerly desire the greater gifts"* (1 Corinthians 12:31). *"Follow the way of love and eagerly desire spiritual gifts, especially the gift of prophecy"* (1 Corinthians 14:1). *"Since you are eager to have spiritual gifts, try to excel in gifts that build up the church"* (1 Corinthians 14:12). *"What then shall we say, brothers? When you come together, everyone has a hymn, or a word of instruction, a revelation, a tongue or an interpretation. All of these must be done for the strengthening of the church"* (1 Corinthians 14:26). Some people believe that the gifts of the Spirit just somehow fall out of the sky at the right moment when needed and that we have no say in how they are developed or released in our lives. Yet the Scriptures are quite clear that we should pursue and seek out spiritual gifts. It is okay to ask for them! It is in accordance with the will of God that we should both anticipate and chase after them. We are meant to trust that if God wants to use anyone in the ministry of spiritual gifts, He certainly wants to use us! At the same time, Paul also calls us to deeply explore the motivations of our hearts. There is certainly a need for spiritual gifts and powerful Spirit encounters in the ministry of the Church, but we should never shy away from being brutally honest about why we want to

see these gifts in action. The building up and strengthening of others must remain our primary goal. How are spiritual gifts deployed in your church? How do they serve to benefit others and the body of believers as a whole? Are your church members actively seeking spiritual gifts and asking for them to increase? What could help encourage them to do so?

5. **Spiritual gifts and other displays of the Spirit's presence and power are rendered pointless unless they are ministered from a heart of genuine love and compassion.** *"And now I will show you the most excellent way. If I speak in the tongues of men and of angels, but have not love, I am only a resounding gong or a clanging cymbal. If I have the gift of prophecy and can fathom all mysteries and all knowledge, and if I have a faith that can move mountains, but have not love, I am nothing. If I give all I possess to the poor and surrender my body to the flames, but do not have love, I gain nothing"* (1 Corinthians 12:31-13:3). Particularly in Pentecostal and Charismatic church gatherings, there can be a temptation for our services to become an ever-increasing spectacle. If the Spirit of God moved in powerful and astounding ways during the last meeting, do we subtly believe that we need to "top" that in the next meeting? We might verbalize that we just want to see more and more people reached for the kingdom of God and delivered from their heavy burdens. That certainly is the right thing to say, yet is it entirely honest? What if God began moving powerfully in this way in the church down the street? Would we support that work? Would we celebrate it? Or are we driven by a competitive mindset that secretly hopes to corner the market on displays of Spirit power in the hope that our own church or ministry might somehow advance instead? Do we privately yearn to be publicly perceived and recognized as God's anointed person of the hour who has thereby become the all-important catalyst for the success of the ministry? God forbid, and Lord help us! This is not the way of love. *"Love is patient, love is kind. It does not envy, it does not boast, it is not proud. It is not rude, it is not self-seeking"* (1 Corinthians 13:4-5). Love will always make the decision to seek the good of others first and foremost. If genuine love for both God and others ever ceases to be our primary directive, then the ministry of the church is ultimately brought to naught and spiritual gifts are rendered useless, no matter how powerful they might otherwise seem in the moment.

6. It is possible to develop and grow in the deployment of spiritual gifts with practice and experience over the course of a lifetime.
"Since you are eager to have spiritual gifts, try to excel in gifts that build up the church. For this reason anyone who speaks in a tongue should pray that he may interpret what he says" (1 Corinthians 14:12-13). When it comes to earthly talents and skills, we easily understand the concept of growth. A healthy child will first crawl, then walk, and then run with practice and the passage of time. Some, with training and focus, will also go on to become great athletes. This Scripture seems to suggest that a similar process exists when it comes to divine enablement by the Spirit of God. Paul tells us not only to be eager for spiritual gifts, but also to "try to excel." This suggests growth, development, and advancement with exercise and experience. As one gift is utilized, others should be sought as well. Will any one person exhibit all spiritual gifts? No, and this mindset should not be our expectation. God has designed the Church to need each of the individual members. Yet, this verse commands us to *"desire the greater gifts"* (1 Corinthians 12:31). How are congregation members encouraged to pursue spiritual gifts? What opportunities are given to them to utilize them during church gatherings? How are they taught and encouraged to practice them in settings beyond the church gatherings?

7. There is a definite time and place for speaking in tongues when the church comes together, but it should not replace sound instruction.
"I thank God that I speak in tongues more than all of you. But in the church I would rather speak five intelligible words to instruct others than ten thousand words in a tongue" (1 Corinthians 14:18-19). The gift of tongues in the life of a believer will have a powerful impact. We explored this in detail back in chapter 4, and there is no need to repeat that information here. However, when it comes to benefiting the Church as a whole when it meets together, Paul emphasizes the importance of instruction and teaching that can be understood with the mind. This would include both prophetic utterances empowered by the Spirit of God and Spirit-empowered preaching and teaching. At all times, the proclamation of the Gospel must occupy a central place in the overall message of the Church. The deployment of spiritual gifts should serve that priority. Of course, we can sometimes observe a pendulum swing in the opposite direction where

spiritual gifts are downplayed or hidden away in the life and ministry of the church so as to not "scare off" those who are otherwise uninitiated and unfamiliar. This too is an error. Paul writes, *"Be eager to prophesy, and do not forbid speaking in tongues"* (1 Corinthians 14:39). Every aspect of the ministry of the Spirit in the Church has its rightful and necessary place. How does this balance in your church ministry occur? What are the purpose and role of speaking in tongues when believers gather together in your setting? Is there a place for prophecy? Interpretation of tongues? What about other spiritual gifts? Healing? Miracles? What else? How do the preaching and teaching reflect the priorities of the Scripture and the cause of the Gospel?

8. **At all times humility in ministry must remain a top priority.** *"Did the word of God originate with you? Or are you the only people it has reached? If anyone thinks he is a prophet or spiritually gifted, let him acknowledge that what I am writing to you is the Lord's command"* (1 Corinthians 14:36-37). The supernatural move of the Spirit through the life of any believer is never meant to bring prestige to any one certain individual. Rather, the goal is to point others to the Lord and strengthen the entire church. In an orchestra, each instrumentalist certainly has a particular role to play but only as it serves the overall piece of music. If one part begins to unduly overshadow the sound of the others or if one instrument starts to go off on its own playing for itself, the concert could be ruined! The same is true in the church. When spiritual gifts are sought as some kind of personal badge of honor or viewed competitively by church members, love has fallen by the wayside and the ministry is rendered worthless. God gives grace to the humble, but He resists the proud! Every member of the body serves a vital function, and no member should be exalted over the others. *"As it is, there are many parts, but one body. The eye cannot say to the hand, 'I don't need you!' And the head cannot say to the feet, 'I don't need you!' . . . If one part suffers, every part suffers with it; if one part is honored, every part rejoices with it. Now you are the body of Christ, and each one of you is a part of it"* (1 Corinthians 12:20-21, 26-27). How does your church practice humility? How do they engage in active preference toward one another and mutual service? In the practice of spiritual gifts, how is that humility prioritized and pursued?

These guidelines make it clear that in the ministry of the Church spiritual gifts should indeed be sought after and utilized, but their use should never become an end unto itself. At all times, the ministry of spiritual gifts must rather serve the common good, the strengthening of the Church, and the proclamation of the Gospel. In addition, these gifts should also showcase the Father's love. How we conduct ministry is as important as the ministry itself. *"But everything should be done in a fitting and orderly way"* (1 Corinthians 14:40).

TEST EVERYTHING

Paul's instruction to the Corinthians demonstrates the balanced approach of embracing an eager and zealous pursuit of Spirit-empowered ministry and not letting go of the essential moorings that keep the Church centered in its mission and calling. This is a balance that Paul demonstrated throughout his years of ministry from start to finish. While he was in Corinth, he wrote his first epistle to the Thessalonians. In chapter 5 of that letter, he offered some final instructions for the church, including *"Do not put out the Spirit's fire; do not treat prophecies with contempt. Test everything. Hold on to the good. Avoid every kind of evil"* (5: 19-22). His words remind us that the ministry of the Spirit must be vigorously sought out and embraced. At the same time, that pursuit must be continually evaluated and reviewed. This is not because of any error or fallibility on the part of the Spirit (of course not!). But it is certainly because we can be all too easily led by our flesh and by mere human reasoning. How do we test prophecies? How do we ensure that our pursuit of supernatural ministry remains healthy? It all comes back to our mission and calling. Do prophetic utterances serve the advancement of the Gospel? Is there a common good that is easily discerned? Does the long-term fruit of supernatural occurrences seem biblical and right? We must be willing to ask hard questions and adjust when necessary, in order to come back into alignment with the guidelines of Scripture as we hold on to the good and reject every kind of evil.

Many, many years later, after he was imprisoned in Rome and near the end of his life, Paul wrote to encourage Timothy, who at that time was serving in pastoral leadership at the church in Ephesus. His second letter to Timothy gives us Paul's final written words. In the opening chapter, he reminded Timothy to *"fan into flame the gift of God . . . . For God did not give us a spirit of timidity, but a spirit of power, of love and of self-discipline"* (2 Timothy 1:6-7). The work of the

Spirit in our lives and the use of the spiritual gifts He gives us are meant to be encouraged, strengthened, and pursued to greater impact and demonstration. The flame of the Spirit is meant to grow and increase! For those who have ears to hear, Paul's Spirit-empowered voice expands from Timothy to each of us. May we fan into flame the gift of the Spirit more and more and more, even as we work to simultaneously honor the guidelines and directives of the Word.

PAUSE AND REFLECT:

Having read the guidelines for ministry derived from chapters 12-14 of 1 Corinthians, let's probe a bit deeper. Grab your Bible and read those texts anew. Ask the Lord to give you fresh eyes. Then reread the guidelines presented in this chapter. What personal answers do you have to the questions asked with each guideline? Take time to write them out in a journal.

Follow the same process with your leadership and staff in a joint gathering. This may require more than one session. Lead an open conversation as you process each guideline and discuss answers to the questions.

In what ways were the thoughts and responses of your leadership and staff similar to yours? In what ways were they different? What insights did you glean from each other? What areas of agreement rose to the surface? Were there any areas of contention or confusion? What steps might you consider as you all work together to better align with the teachings of Scripture?

The eight guidelines presented in this chapter are by no means the only guidelines to be found in the biblical text. What additional guidelines, if any, would you add based on the Scripture? Do you disagree with or have a different perspective from what these guidelines present?

Does your church have a process for testing prophecies or for reviewing the habits and traditions of how ministry is conducted in your setting? What corrections or changes might need to take place? What aspects need to be better encouraged?

Chapter 9
The Ministry of the Spirit and Extra-Biblical Phenomena

To this point, we have explored the ministry of the Holy Spirit as it took place in numerous New Testament churches. The incredible miracle accounts have served to undergird a missional emphasis of proclaiming the Gospel message to lost and hurting people and to demonstrate the love of God in tangible ways. The Spirit's ministry in these churches provides a tremendous series of examples for us today. We read the Scriptures and find both inspiration and practical methods as the Lord uses His Word to increase our faith to trust Him for supernatural ministry today. From speaking in tongues, interpretation of tongues, and prophecy to miracles, healings, deliverance from demons, and more, everything about the biblical accounts indicates that what the Spirit has done before, He will yet continue.

Nothing in Scripture indicates that the display of supernatural Spirit-empowered ministry has ceased. On the contrary, two thousand years of church history since those early days have revealed that the Lord is certainly still moving in miraculous ways to bring people to Christ and to advance the kingdom of God. Written accounts of believers being filled with the Spirit and speaking in tongues can be found in every age. The same can be said regarding the gift of prophecy. Martin Luther affirmed the importance of spiritual gifts by including them in the fourth verse of his famous hymn *"A Mighty Fortress is our God"* (written around the year 1527), as he taught us to sing,

> *That Word above all earthly powers,*
> *no thanks to them abideth;*
> *the Spirit and the gifts are ours,*
> *through Him who with us sideth!*

Luther's point throughout the song is that the enemy has been overcome by Christ Jesus and believers can help bring deliverance wherever it is yet needed by the supernatural gifts of the Spirit. Praise be to God!

Throughout church history, it is also apparent that the Spirit has worked in ways that we do not necessarily see in Scripture. People have been known to suddenly and uncontrollably tremble while seemingly experiencing the ministry of the Spirit. Others cry out in dramatic fashion. Some become exuberant and begin to dance. Some have been known to twitch and jerk as if having spasms. Still others have occasionally had visions. Many have suddenly fallen to the ground, finding themselves without the strength to stand. There are stories of meeting rooms being filled with visible manifestations of the glory of God like a cloud. In recent decades, there have also been stories of what is claimed to be golden dust suddenly appearing on those in worship or receiving prayer. Such events and stories only scratch the surface of the many ways that God has miraculously worked in various settings, and they remain a wonder. What are we to do with them? Does the Holy Spirit really move in these ways?

God is the God of the miraculous. There are no limits to what He can do. Though we might not always immediately understand the purposes of such occurrences, it remains true that the Lord's ways are not our ways. The Holy Spirit can certainly work in ways that defy our experience and expectation. However, at the same time, it is also true that people can become overly gullible and foolish as they get caught up in the moment. Some ministers and ministries have even resorted to trickery and the creation of false experiences in an effort to draw a crowd and manipulate them. Not everything that is claimed to be a divine work of God is a divine work of God. There is a necessary balance that must be maintained between being zealous for the supernatural move of the Spirit while discerning what is true and right, and having nothing to do with what is false and deceptive. To that end, may we be ever eager and receive with joy the work of the Spirit, and may we remain ever centered in the Scripture as we seek out truth and build a foundation for a growing faith in the Lord.

CATEGORIZING THE WORK OF THE SPIRIT

If both church history and contemporary experience contain examples not only of supernatural workings of the Spirit but also of false and deceptive practices, how can we best discern the true nature of what we may be encountering? How can we safeguard our churches from what is false without unduly quenching the Holy Spirit, who may be working in ways that we simply have not previously seen? It may be helpful to consider three categories by which we can classify various experiences that can occur in ministry: *biblical*, *unbiblical*, and *extra-biblical*.

Biblical happenings and occurrences of the supernatural work of the Holy Spirit are exactly what this category name suggests. If something is biblical, we should be able to clearly point to the exact verses in the Bible where similar occurrences took place. In the Scriptures, people prophesied through the anointing of the Spirit. They spoke in tongues. They ministered healing. They performed miracles and the like. Such actions are *biblical*. The first eight chapters of this book are intended to focus on biblical examples of the ministry of the Spirit so that we might thrive in our relationship with Him!

A second category would be acts and occurrences that are *unbiblical*. These would include supernatural activities and experiences that are clearly forbidden by the Scriptures. A few dramatic examples would

> **PAUSE AND REFLECT:**
>
> In what ways has your church been impacted by supernatural ministry? What marvelous triumphs have you observed? Have there been any associated difficulties? Why do you think that is?
>
> What **biblical** workings of the Spirit are also observed in your church? Are there any biblical examples and activities that are not taking place?
>
> Have your church members experienced supernatural occurrences that are perhaps best described as **extra-biblical?** How does the church react to such events? What is your congregation taught regarding extra-biblical activity? How do such occurrences serve the overall mission of the Church?
>
> Have you ever had to address **unbiblical** supernatural happenings in your church? What examples have you observed in other places? What actions would you recommend to a ministry faced with unbiblical activity among its members?

include trying to guide one's life and ascertain the future via the movements of stars and planets (Deuteronomy 4:19; Isaiah 47:13-15), the practice of sorcery and witchcraft (Deuteronomy 18:10), and attempting to communicate with and/or contact the dead (Deuteronomy 18:11-13). Also included would be attempts to utilize spiritual gifts for selfish gain, especially when embracing fakery or exaggeration. Other *unbiblical* activity would be that which is not necessarily addressed in the Scriptures specifically but is clearly sourced in practices outside the scope of Christian belief. The pursuit of out-of-body experiences via astral projection, interactions with incorporeal "spirit-guides" who supposedly provide wisdom and direction in life, and the utilization of Tarot cards (and the like) are not practices addressed in the Bible, but they are actions associated with the occult and with New Age practices and beliefs. The same holds true for trying to capture the mystical energy of crystals, using meditation to tap into a universal cosmic consciousness, or inducing hallucinogenic states via drugs to obtain divine revelation, and a countless number of other unseemly practices. All of these are attempts to activate or manipulate spiritual forces without submission to God or His Word. It should go without saying that all unbiblical occurrences of apparent supernatural power should be immediately avoided at all costs. Such things are great sins and lead to horrific errors and terrible consequences.

Our third category, *extra-biblical* phenomena, however, are those happenings that seem to supernaturally occur in the context of Christian ministry but may not be specifically addressed in the Scriptures at all. They are not in opposition to the teachings and examples found in the Bible, and neither are they sourced in practices stemming from other belief systems. They rather fall into a broad category of surprising "signs and wonders" that lack a clear and exact biblical example. Yet in the aftermath, people bear godly fruit and experience godly transformation. What are we to do with such occurrences? As described earlier, they can happen with surprising regularity.

An attempt to analyze all the possible *extra-biblical* experiences that have taken place throughout church history or even in more recent Pentecostal and Charismatic settings is more than can be done in this volume. The subject is simply too broad! However, let us consider one example of *extra-biblical* Spirit phenomena that has been commonly experienced by many throughout the world both currently and in times past: "falling under the power (of God)" or being "slain in the Spirit." By working through the categorization of being *biblical, unbiblical,* or *extra-biblical* with this common occurrence, we can perhaps embrace a process of evaluation that can serve as a guideline for how to approach other phenomena if and when they occur.

DISCERNING *EXTRA-BIBLICAL* PHENOMENA: "FALLING UNDER THE POWER"

Perhaps you have seen the following scenario in a church service, on the television, on the internet, or somewhere else. People come forward to receive prayer and then sometime during the process, they suddenly fall to the ground. Across Pentecostal and Charismatic history, these types of incidents have sometimes been referred to as being "slain in the Spirit" or "falling under the power" of the Holy Spirit. The former Roman Catholic priest Francis McNutt preferred the terms "resting in the Spirit" or being "overcome by the Spirit" as he felt the other descriptions were unduly dramatic and potentially threatening. Regardless of the terminology, what is really happening? Is God really knocking people over for some reason only known to Him? Is this truly some kind of supernatural work of the Spirit? Is it, perhaps, merely a form of emotionalism? Are those who are ministering physically pushing people to the ground, or are they somehow inducing some kind of psychological experience through the power of suggestion and/or mass hypnosis? Is this a relatively modern event and part of some weird, religious fad that has simply persisted over the past few decades?

For some folks, this sudden loss of strength seems to happen in dramatic fashion. Some fall backward, some forward, and some sideways. Some bodies go stiff as a board while others crumble into a heap. Some people may lie on the ground for a long time while others get back up quickly. Some tremble, jerk, twitch, and shake as they fall, even rolling across the floor. Some may weep, groan, and cry out while others burst into sudden laughter. Still others may grow quiet and even begin to rest peacefully. Sometimes all of this can be happening simultaneously in a single gathering. What are we to make of such things? As we read through the Scripture, it is apparent that we could eliminate the *unbiblical* category. There is nothing in the Bible that seems to prohibit or to speak against such occurrences. Neither do they seem to be unique to any pagan or false belief system. On the other hand, we must also ask, "Is it *biblical*?" Can we find similar activity within the accounts of the Scriptures?

In 2 Chronicles 5:13-14 (and 1 Kings 8:10-11) we find the account of the dedication of the Temple of the Lord by Solomon. After having carried in the Ark of the Covenant, and as the people began to play instruments and sing and give thanks to the Lord, the Scripture tells us that the presence of God came into the room in the form of a thick cloud. One immediate result was that the priests were no longer physically able to continue in their service because they were overcome by the tangible presence of the Lord. In 2 Chronicles 7:3 (NLT), we are also told that when all the people saw this taking place, they *"fell face down on the ground and worshiped and praised the Lord."*

The difficulty with this account is that we are not exactly able to compare apples to apples when we consider modern occurrences of people falling in apparent response to the move of the Spirit. First, it is unclear whether the ancient Israelites who fell to the ground were doing so as a voluntary act of worship or as an involuntary result of being in the presence of the Lord. Most Bible translations seem to side with the idea that they voluntarily bowed or knelt. Additionally, it does not seem that a thick, dark cloud is visibly filling the room in the vast majority of our ministry settings today. (Although there have been a few isolated stories of this taking place in various locales through the years, it would be nice to have some hard evidence of such occurrences.) At the very least, the story does seem to provide a minimal degree of biblical precedent for an observable physical reaction in the human body as God made Himself known via the power and presence of the Holy Spirit.

The prophet Daniel described a couple of instances when he lost strength and fell to the ground in the presence of an angel. In his eighth chapter, Daniel describes a complicated divine and highly symbolic vision he received from the Lord. After Daniel had received that vision, the angel Gabriel suddenly appeared with an interpretation from God to help the prophet understand and process what he had seen. Daniel wrote that when Gabriel approached, he (Daniel) *"was terrified and fell prostrate"* (Daniel 8:17). After the encounter he also indicated that he *"was exhausted and lay ill for several days"* (verse 27). Sometime later, the prophet had another vision of an angel appearing to him. Of that encounter, he stated, *"I had no strength left, my face turned deathly pale and I was helpless. Then I heard him speaking, and as I listened to him, I fell into a deep sleep, my face to the ground"* (Daniel 10:8-9). With both of Daniel's accounts, we again see a connection between the presence of the Lord (this time as expressed through an angel and a vision) and a reaction in the physical body, though there are also still some differences when compared to what is typically seen in Charismatic ministry settings today.

In the New Testament, Saul of Tarsus was suddenly and involuntarily thrown to the ground when he encountered a bright, supernatural light from heaven and heard the voice of Jesus suddenly speak to him from out of nowhere while he was on his way to Damascus to persecute Christians (Acts 9:1-9 and Acts 26:12-18). That encounter changed his life forever. In addition, the apostle John also mentioned that he himself experienced a surprising involuntary response in his own body when the Lord Jesus appeared before him in all His glory. John wrote, *"When I saw him, I fell at His feet as though dead"* (Revelation 1:17). Again, both accounts present us with a sudden bodily reaction to the presence of the Lord.

Other scriptural accounts of similar phenomena concern those who are described as demonized. On numerous occasions, people afflicted by demons would suddenly be thrown to the ground or into convulsions in the presence of Jesus. Mark 3:11, Mark 9:20, and Luke 8:28 are a few examples of this. Of course, in these accounts this condition of "falling" was part of the person's ongoing ailment as they were being tormented by the demon (perhaps something akin to epilepsy?), and these Scriptures note the events associated with each individual's deliverance.

Reviewing these accounts, while there seems to be biblical similitude to the "falling under the power" that is sometimes observed today, the comparison is not perfect. We do not find exact accounts of people inexplicably falling to the ground after receiving prayer in an apparent reaction to the presence of the Holy Spirit. In the strictest terms, then, such activity does not seem to be necessarily *biblical*. Does that mean that such phenomena today cannot be of God? By no means! Nothing shows this to be necessarily *unbiblical* either! Certainly God can do what He wants. Yet, without clear examples of such activity in the Scripture, being "slain in the Spirit" is probably best categorized as *extra-biblical* phenomena. Is that good? In other words, does it serve a biblical purpose even if it does not directly include a biblical example? To help us decide, we should also consider what we might learn from the examples of church history.

A TIMELINE OF SPIRIT-EMPOWERED MINISTRY

Being so-called "slain in the Spirit" is often viewed as a fairly modern experience and commonly associated with the Charismatic movement starting in the late 1960s and early '70s. There is no question that the availability of the internet in our technologically advanced era has also allowed this experience to be observed by many who have never stepped foot into a Pentecostal or Charismatic gathering. When we look back at church history, however, we find that the act of falling to the ground while receiving prayer in apparent reaction to the presence of God is not without precedent. It is definitely not confined to the modern era at all.

Spiritual phenomena and Charismatic activities such as healings, miracles, prophecies, and speaking in tongues are documented multiple times during the first three hundred years of Christianity. During this period, believers gathered primarily in home settings, and such supernatural activity flourished throughout the body of Christ. With the rise of Constantine and the institutionalizing of the Church, however, we see a rapid decline in the discussion of charismata in the writings of the Church. In fact, such "giftings" eventually became reserved for only the local bishops (along with other particular religious functions, such as the authority to read the Scriptures and to administer holy communion). It wasn't long, then, before the occurrence of such activity seemed to all but disappear from the historical record, at least for a while. Some theologians would eventually argue that the supernatural activity of the Spirit in the life of the Church must have ceased altogether and was not meant to continue. Interestingly, however, as the now legalized Church became institutionalized with buildings and a hierarchy, others began to reject those imposed structures and instead started various monastic orders as a way to preserve what they understood to be an actualized, living faith in God. It is through their records that we find a written preservation of the supernatural activity of the Spirit in the experience of those who followed Christ.

One of the first historical documentations of being "slain in the Spirit" is found in the early 14th century. It occurred through the ministry of Vincent Ferrer, who was part of the Dominicans, a Catholic order founded by Saint Dominic. Dominic and his contemporary, Francis of Assisi, were both recognized by the Church as regularly demonstrating charismatic giftings, including tongues, miracles, healings, and even raisings from the dead! Living almost two hundred years later, Vincent Ferrer was known for preaching and teaching with incredible results all across Europe as many became disciples of Jesus. It is said that during his preaching, overpowering sobs would rise from the congregations. Everywhere he preached, countless conversions and amazing miracles were recounted along with numerous reports that many suddenly "fainted." Though these accounts were written over six hundred years ago, they bear a striking similarity to modern day experiences of being "overcome by the Spirit."

During the sixteenth century, the Anabaptists became highly persecuted for their belief that water baptism was for believers only and that infants should therefore not be baptized. That description is a huge simplification, but a detailed history of the Anabaptists exceeds the intentions and scope of this writing. The persecution they received caused them to often meet secretly in homes as well as in forests and in fields. At their gatherings, they were known for reading the Bible aloud and for asking that the same Spirit who had been known by the early Church would come upon them as well. Though the widespread nature of typical charismatic activity among this group during that time frame is debated, it was certainly not unusual for those Anabaptists to "fall under the power" and to speak in tongues during their gatherings.

The Huguenots of the seventeenth century were severely persecuted by Louis XIV. While many fled France during this time, large numbers chose to remain and concentrated themselves in the Cevennes Mountains. They became known as the "French Prophets" because of what seemed to be a tremendous outpouring of the presence and power of the Holy Spirit in their midst. Dr. Eddie Hyatt, in his book *2000 Years of Charismatic Christianity*, reports that tongues, visions, prophecies, and other supernatural phenomena were common among them. In one gathering it was said that they "fell on their backs, they shut their eyes, they heaved with their breast, they remained a while in trances, and coming out of them with twitchings, they utter'd all that came into their mouths."[1]

The eighteenth century is noted for the powerful prayer gatherings of the Moravians. Fervent times of intercession were known to last all night long, and spontaneous yearnings for prayer would happen in children and adults alike. On August 19, 1727, a Moravian congregation had gathered in Herrnhut, Germany, for Sunday worship. Around noon that day, the pastor was "overwhelmed by the presence of the Lord and fell to the floor. The entire congregation, overwhelmed by the Spirit and presence of the Lord, then sank to the floor with him. The service continued until midnight with prayer and singing, weeping and supplication."[2] This sounds like the revival meetings of our day!

It is said that the renowned John Wesley experienced something similar during his ministry. His meetings were marked by strong preaching, healings, deliverances, and experiences such as falling, trembling, roaring, crying, and laughing. During the rise of the Methodist movement, these experiences spread throughout many local parishes under a variety of leaders including John Berridge, Thomas Walsh, and John Fletcher, among others. Similar accounts were also noted under the ministry of Wesley's friend George Whitefield and his contemporary, Jonathan Edwards. Historians note this time by calling it the First Great Awakening.

It seems that the exact phrase "slain in the Spirit" may have originated during the nineteenth century. Presbyterian pastor James McGready led a series of small congregations in Kentucky. In 1800, after four years of regular congregational prayer and fasting for revival, the Red River Church that he served had an encounter with God that resulted in meetings that went on for days. It drew in many outsiders, including both unbelievers and Christians, from a variety of other places and other congregations. On the final day of meetings, Methodist minister John McGhee gave an exhortation near the end of the gathering, amidst a time of prayer and weeping. Historian Charles A. Johnson records in a publication called *The Frontier Camp Meeting* that McGhee declared this:

> **I exhorted them to let the Lord Omnipotent reign in their hearts and submit to Him and their souls should live. Many broke silence. The woman in the east end of the house shouted tremendously. I left the pulpit to go to her. Several spoke to me, "You know these people Presbyterian are much for order, they will not bear the confusion, go back and be quiet." I turned to go back and was near falling, the power of God was strong upon me. I turned again, and losing sight of fear of man, I went through the house shouting and exhorting with all possible ecstasy and energy and the floor was soon covered by the "slain."[3]**

In the aftermath of the preaching, all kinds of people had been suddenly falling under the power of God as they submitted themselves to the lordship of Christ. The fervor from these meetings soon spread across Kentucky and beyond, sparking what became known as the Second Great Awakening.

Such activity began to become more and more typical of various ministries throughout the U.S., including that of revivalist Charles G. Finney. Of one particular meeting in Rome, New York, Finney wrote that as he was praying near the end of the gathering, "a young man . . . being one of the first young men in that place, so nearly fainted, that he fell upon some young men who stood near him; and then all of them partially swooned away, and fell together."[4]

The nineteenth and early twentieth centuries would be marked by numerous "revivals" conducted by a variety of ministries across the United States and Europe that all featured demonstrative activity attributed to the supernatural work of the Spirit of God, including both the Welsh and Scottish revivals and also the often-discussed Azusa Street "outpouring" of 1906 in California. This latter event is considered the launch of what would become the Pentecostal movement. The references to Spirit activity, including occurrences of individuals being "overcome" by the power of God, became widespread and normative in these settings. The Pentecostal movement then, in turn, fathered the Charismatic movement in which people across a wide variety of denominations (including both mainline Protestants and Catholics) began to have supernatural encounters with God with repeated experiences of losing strength and falling under the power of the Spirit. Such activity was eventually brought into the light of mainstream public consciousness through the much publicized and influential ministry of Kathryn Kuhlman during the 1960s and '70s. She almost single-handedly popularized the expression "slain in the Spirit" to describe those who would fall during worship or when receiving prayer. That awareness continues today, worldwide, through countless ministries conducted by numerous churches and ministers around the globe.

This history demonstrates that these experiences of being "slain in the Spirit," as well as numerous other physical responses to the presence of God (both voluntary and perhaps involuntary), are by no means unique to the modern era. We see this occurring over and over throughout the history of the Church.

It seems to be a series and pattern of regular occurrences as people cried out to the Lord, repeatedly documented for more than seven hundred years and certainly implied in the centuries before. It may be *extra-biblical*, but it is clearly not *unbiblical*.

WHAT PURPOSE DOES THIS SERVE?

The big question, of course, is why does this kind of phenomena occur at all? There are likely a variety of reasons. It may very well be that many times people lose strength during moments of ministry as a direct result of some supernatural activity by the Holy Spirit. Whether it takes place because of some specific work of transformation that the Lord wants to accomplish, or whether it is the physical reaction by a particular person who has come into some kind of tangible contact with the power of God, it seems to be a wonder ultimately resulting from the work and ministry of the Holy Spirit. Some people may be very aware of what God is specifically doing in them during these moments (some reportedly have visions; some have a great sense of God's healing, either physical or emotional), while many others may not have any specific understanding, but perhaps only a general yet powerful sense of the presence of God. In the end, the experience serves to direct people to the lordship of Christ and to minister to their needs in a powerful and profound way.

This description does not preclude, however, the fact that certain people may fall over for a variety of other reasons which may not be so divinely inspired. It is conceivable that some may fall out of a sense of religious frenzy, wanting God to do something powerful in their lives. This could happen either deliberately or even subconsciously. It could also be that some falling is the result of demonized people reacting to the manifested presence and power of the Holy Spirit. In this case, the falling could either be a distraction from, or a response to, the deliverance taking place by the Spirit, depending on any number of variables. Our finite minds want to define these experiences in exact categories with specific boundaries when it seems more likely that the activity taking place could be as varied as the individuals themselves.

One of the spiritual gifts specifically listed by Paul is "distinguishing" between spirits (1 Corinthians 12:10). Wise leadership should seek the Lord regarding the growth and use of this gift so that the Holy Spirit can guide them in how to respond to such a variety of experiences. Those who may simply be engaged in fleshly exercise can be corrected either at the moment or perhaps at another time suitable for all those involved. Those displaying demonic manifestations should be offered deliverance and freedom. In every case, however, we should be careful to not decisively dismiss or judge what's happening in others based merely on our limited and momentary view. May we be led by and walk in step with the Spirit at all times. Additionally, we should not form doctrines on the basis of ecstatic experiences. Rather, we should continually return to a study of the Scriptures and allow them to frame our theology and practice. We should long for long-term fruitfulness demonstrated by genuine personal transformation evidenced over time.

Leadership has a responsibility in these matters to consider what best serves the work of love in these situations. If there is a sense that some people might swoon in moments of ministry, how can we help to lovingly serve them? Many churches incorporate people as "catchers." One of the goals in such moments is the safety of all involved. Occasionally the remark is made, "Well, if the Spirit is ministering to people in this way, certainly God will protect them." That may sound reasonable, but not when we realize that people may be "overcome" for any variety of reasons, spiritual and otherwise. While it is a good idea to have others present to help, it might also be advisable to have people sit down to receive ministry or perhaps simply lie down on the floor from the beginning. Church leaders should have robust conversations concerning how loving service can best be implemented in their setting as it concerns these kinds of ministry moments. There is real value, however, in considering how to reduce what is unnecessarily dramatic. May we focus on what God is doing first and foremost!

WHAT TO DO WITH EXTRA-BIBLICAL PHENOMENA

Whatever extra-biblical activity that may appear in the context of Church ministry, it should never be allowed to become an end unto itself. It should never become the focal point of ministry. The directive of Jesus is to *"go and make disciples of all nations, baptizing them in the name of the Father and of the Son and of the Holy Spirit"* (Matthew 28:19). The highest priority activity that we must pursue is to love the Lord our God with all our heart, soul, and mind and then to love our neighbors as we love ourselves (Matthew 22:37-39). While Paul tells us to be zealous for spiritual gifts, that zeal cannot come at the expense of love or take the focus away from the mission and calling of the Church.

Is it possible to become so enamored with extra-biblical supernatural phenomena that we can lose our way? The answer to that is a most definite and unfortunate "yes." It is certainly possible. In some circles today, there is pushback among certain ministries concerning this truth. They will even boldly proclaim that it is impossible for a heart that loves the Lord to be led astray, declaring that they have more confidence in the Lord to lead them into all truth than in the devil's ability to bring deception. This sounds noble but is actually contrary to the Scriptures which call us to continual scrutiny and review. In his first letter to the Corinthians, Paul wrote, *"So, if you think you are standing firm, be careful that you don't fall!"* (1 Corinthians 10:12). In chapters 12-14 of that same letter, he goes on to give careful guidance and correction to the church in Corinth even though they had become well experienced in the workings of the Spirit. Moreover, Paul primarily wrote his letter to the Galatians in order to correct them for falling into deep and serious error and deception (Galatians 1:6-9, 3:1). If those believers could be led astray, so can we.

When it comes to the supernatural move of the Spirit and potential extra-biblical phenomena, all judgments should be made not by mere appearance in the moment, but by the long-term evidence of transformation. In addressing how to discern what is false from what is true, Jesus once remarked, *"By their fruit you will recognize them"* (Matthew 7:16). The goal of a supernatural Spirit-empowered ministry is not to make spectacular signs and wonders happen for their own sake; it is to make faithful, long-lasting, love-filled disciples of Jesus as we encounter a broken and hurting world. The fruit of the Spirit in the life of those experiencing Spirit phenomena should be increasing. There should be a heart longing to pursue God-honoring practices in addition to a determined turning away from sin. Over time, the evidence of transformation by the Spirit should be more and more obvious! Along the way, as we walk with the Lord and learn to thrive in the Spirit, let's cling to what is *biblical*, run from what is *unbiblical*, and joyously but carefully embrace what is *extra-biblical* as it serves the cause of Christ, even as we continually study, conform to the Word, and evaluate healthy fruitfulness over the passage of time. To God be the glory!

PAUSE AND REFLECT:

What did you think of the scriptural assessment of "falling under the power"? Do you agree with the conclusion that such activity in the Church today may be extra-biblical, but not unbiblical? What danger might there be in trying to find "proof-text" verses to validate spiritual experiences in order to prove them as being biblical?

What is your reaction to the historical information regarding "falling under the power of the Spirit"? Should church history have a bearing on our understanding of how to address extra-biblical phenomena? What other considerations should play a part?

Have you ever experienced the need to assess apparent divine workings of the Spirit in order to confront confusion or error? What is the balance between rejoicing over sudden supernatural moments in ministry and searching the Scriptures to ensure everything is biblical and right?

How might chasing after the miraculous for its own sake lead to error? Are there certain practices in ministry that tend to be error prone or susceptible to deception? Discuss with your leaders what those might be? How can right practices be developed without "quenching" the Spirit?

---

[1] Eddie L. Hyatt, *2000 Years of Charismatic Christianity* (Dallas: Hyatt International Ministries, 1998), 94.

[2] Hyatt, *2000 Years of Charismatic Christianity*, 104.

[3] Charles A. Johnson, *The Frontier Camp Meeting* (Dallas, TX: Southern Methodist University, 1955), 35.

[4] Charles G. Finney, *An Autobiography* (Old Tappan, NJ: Revell, 1908), 20.

Epilogue
Further Up and Further In

One day Jesus was traveling with His disciples, and they came to the region of Caesarea Philippi. This was a city rebuilt by Philip the Tetrarch, one of the sons of Herod the Great. Herod had previously built the great seaport of Caesarea on the shores of the Mediterranean in tribute to Caesar, and Philip wanted to establish his own city to honor Caesar as well. Before being renamed by Philip, the city was called Paneas because it contained an ornate temple, situated along the base of a massive cliff wall, that was dedicated to the god Pan. Terrible things happened at that pagan temple site, including child sacrifice. It was known as a place of great evil, and the locals both in antiquity and today refer to it as "the gates of hell." Let us consider anew what happened when Jesus and His disciples arrived there.

> He asked his disciples, "Who do people say the Son of Man is?"
>
> They replied, "Some say John the Baptist; others say Elijah; and still others, Jeremiah or one of the prophets."
>
> "But what about you?" he asked. "Who do you say I am?"
>
> Simon Peter answered, "You are the Christ, the Son of the living God."
>
> Jesus replied, "Blessed are you, Simon son of Jonah, for this was not revealed to you by man, but by my Father in heaven. And I tell you that you are Peter, and on this rock I will build my church, and the gates of Hades will not overcome it" (Matthew 16:13-18).

What an incredible revelation this was! Peter had declared that Jesus was the Messiah, the Son of God, and Jesus had declared that He was building a Church that the gates of Hades would not be able to overcome. It is a picture of the Church triumphant, ministering in the power and presence of the Lord Himself. This conversation could have happened anywhere, but Jesus chose to have it in the shadow of a pagan temple that stood in opposition to the very purposes of God. That temple was built at the base of an immense rock. The rock upon which Christ is building His Church is far bigger! The Lord is not, and has never been, daunted by the supposed power of the enemy. He, at all times, remains fully confident in who He is and in whom He is causing His Church to be. Sometime later, He promised His disciples that they would receive power when the Holy Spirit came on them, and they would become His witnesses to the very ends of the earth (Acts 1:8). That promise is still being carried out, from one generation to the next, as our victorious Lord continues to build a Church that is vibrant and strong by the power and presence of the Holy Spirit. No matter how dark or demonic this world might seem, it can never overcome the Church that Jesus is building!

The Lord has called us to be a vibrant part of His Church. To that end, He has poured out His Spirit in order that we might have a thriving relationship with Him and walk in the confident love and power that comes from Him. With that in mind, here is another interesting fact about Caesarea Philippi. The same mountain wall that housed the pagan temple also contained an apparently bottomless pit filled with water. It was a natural formation, present within the mountain from long before the pagan temple existed. Furthermore, deep springs from within the mountain burst forth at that site and form the beginning of the Jordan River, which gives life to all the rest of Israel below.

In John 7:37-38, Jesus declared to the crowd, *"If anyone is thirsty, let him come to Me and drink. Whoever believes in Me, as the Scripture has said, streams of living water will flow from within him."* To make sure we truly understand these words, John tells us in verse 39 that Jesus was speaking of the Holy Spirit, who would be poured out to the believers. Though spoken while Jesus was in Jerusalem, His words nonetheless evoke what we find in the geography of Caesarea Philippi. Just as water comes gushing out from the place where He is first recognized as the Son of God and then blesses the nation, so too is the living water of the Spirit meant to spring forth from us and touch the world!

This book is meant to help us experience the presence of God anew. It is intended to expand our thinking and encourage our faith as we embrace a relationship with the Spirit of God. It is also meant to help our churches be places where the ministry of God's Spirit can flow in the midst of healthy teaching and an atmosphere of loving hearts. By no means is this book intended to be any kind of final say regarding the ministry of the Spirit. It is a beginning . . . and perhaps a catalyst for more. May our thirst for the Lord ever increase! May we come to Christ and drink deeply of the living water that He offers us.

We are not meant to simply experience the presence of the Holy Spirit in some sort of momentary mystical or magical way; we are meant to thrive in a lifelong, ever-deepening relationship with Him in which we are continually refined and simultaneously empowered to demonstrate the Father's love and care for the world. Having tasted of Him, may we ever yearn for more. There is more to know, there is more to experience, there is more to enjoy, and there is more to share.

In the last book of his *Chronicles of Narnia* series, *The Last Battle*, C.S. Lewis writes of the end of the age for his fictional world, Narnia. In a fable meant to portray the truths of Scripture, he describes how the old land of Narnia was overtaken by the divine creation of the new Narnia. He mentions that just as there is a difference between a mirror and the real thing, there is a difference between the old land that is going away and the finding of the newly created world to come. In many ways, he paints with words a picture of a life before Christ, without the fullness of the Spirit, and a life in Christ, full of the very Spirit of God. The latter is more real, more alive, more vibrant, more satisfying, and with ever more to be discovered. In the context of Lewis's novel, a majestic unicorn approaches those standing on the periphery of the new Narnia and calls out to them, "I have come home at last! This is my real country! I belong here. This is the land I have been looking for all my life, though I never knew it till now. The reason we loved the old Narnia is that it sometimes looked a little like this. Bree-heehee! Come further up, come further in!"[1]

What a beautiful allegory Lewis provides for us. We were made for a life in the Spirit. The baptism in the Holy Spirit provides us with a foretaste of all the fullness of heaven. As we learn to live by the Spirit, responding to the Word with ongoing submission and obedience and loving the Lord our God with all our heart, soul, and strength, we are ever pointed further up and further in. What are we waiting for? There is so much fullness, joy, and wonder to be found in Him. Let us drink deeply of the living water of the Spirit and embrace all that He wants to do to rescue and redeem the broken and the lost.

What an adventure He has called us to join!

Come … thrive in the Spirit!

---

[1] C.S. Lewis, *The Last Battle*, First Collier Books Edition (New York: Macmillan Publishing Company, 1970), 171.

Made in the USA
Monee, IL
03 August 2023